UNIVERSITY OF NORTH CAROLINA AT CHAPEL HILL
DEPARTMENT OF ROMANCE LANGUAGES

NORTH CAROLINA STUDIES IN THE ROMANCE LANGUAGES AND LITERATURES

ESSAYS; TEXTS, TEXTUAL STUDIES AND TRANSLATIONS; SYMPOSIA

Founder: URBAN TIGNER HOLMES

Distributed by:

UNIVERSITY OF NORTH CAROLINA PRESS
CHAPEL HILL
North Carolina 27514
U.S.A.

NORTH CAROLINA STUDIES IN THE
ROMANCE LANGUAGES AND LITERATURES
Essays
Number 2

CHRÉTIEN'S JEWISH GRAIL
A NEW INVESTIGATION OF THE IMAGERY AND SIGNIFICANCE OF
CHRÉTIEN DE TROYES'S GRAIL EPISODE BASED UPON
MEDIEVAL HEBRAIC SOURCES

PLATE 1. The Simple Son and the Son Who Knows Not How to Ask. A Provençal or Spanish *Haggadah*, 14th Century.

CHRÉTIEN'S JEWISH GRAIL
A NEW INVESTIGATION OF THE IMAGERY AND SIGNIFICANCE OF CHRÉTIEN DE TROYES'S GRAIL EPISODE BASED UPON MEDIEVAL HEBRAIC SOURCES

BY

EUGENE J. WEINRAUB

CHAPEL HILL

NORTH CAROLINA STUDIES IN THE ROMANCE
LANGUAGES AND LITERATURES
U.N.C. DEPARTMENT OF ROMANCE LANGUAGES
1976

Library of Congress Cataloging in Publication Data

Weinraub, Eugene J.
  Chrétien's Jewish grail.

  (North Carolina Studies in the Romance Languages and Literatures; Essays, No. 2)

  Bibliography: p.
  1. Chrestien de Troyes, 12th cent. Perceval le Gallois — Sources. 2. Jews. Liturgy and ritual.
Hagadah — Influence. I. Title. II. Series.
PQ1445.P7W4   841'.1   75-29182
ISBN: 9780807891681

DEPÓSITO LEGAL: V. 616 - 1976

ARTES GRÁFICAS SOLER, S. A. - JÁVEA, 28 - VALENCIA (8) - 1976

For my devoted wife Jocelyne and darling daughter Léora, for my dear parents Jacob and Esther Weinraub and for my beloved mentor Professor Alice M. Colby.

ב"ה

ACKNOWLEDGMENTS

As this study is a continuation of research begun in my doctoral dissertation ("Chrétien's Grail: A Jewish Rite? A New Investigation Based Upon Medieval Hebraic Sources," Cornell University, June 1970),[1] I wish to acknowledge the many kind scholars who generously gave of their time and expertise in aiding me in that first major scholarly achievement as well as in the present endeavor. First the members of my doctoral committee:

Professor Alice M. Colby (Romance Studies, Cornell), who so conscientiously directed my thesis as well as my studies at Cornell. Not only am I indebted to her for my preparation in medieval French literature, but also for the warmth, sympathetic advice, and understanding which she gave me. Her sound bibliographical guidance greatly aided me in my subsequent research and in the preparation of this volume.

Professor Robert A. Hall, Jr. (Linguistics, Cornell), who introduced me to the study of comparative Romance linguistics, who was most helpful with suggestions, and who has served as a pedagogical model for me.

Professor Alfred Ivry (Semitic Languages and Literatures, Cornell), who was more than generous with his time and advice, who gave me linguistic and literary background in Arabic, and who pointed out many exciting paths for my future research.

I am also indebted to Professors Bernhard Blumenkranz (Paris), Pierre Gallais (Poitiers), the late Urban T. Holmes, Jr. (Chapel Hill), Isaac Rabinowitz (Cornell), the late Samuel M. Stern (Oxford), and Haïm Zafrani (Paris), for bibliographical assistance and encouragement.

---

[1] University Microfilms Inc., Ann Arbor, Michigan, Reorder No. 71-1081.

I am grateful to Professors John Freccero (Yale) and Abraham L. Udovitch (Princeton), both formerly of Cornell, for having served on my committee and having been sources of inspiration to me; to Professors David I. Grossvogel and Robert E. Kaske of Cornell, for having attended my Final Examination; and to Professor Juan Bautista Avalle-Arce (Chapel Hill) and the editorial staff of UNCSRLL for their careful reading of my manuscript, for their many useful suggestions, and for their valuable bibliographical aid.

Special thanks are due Brig. Gen. Gad Navon, Deputy Chief Rabbi of the Israel Defense Forces, for his scholarly advice and his most generous co-operation.

I should like to thank the Field of Romance Studies and the Graduate School of Cornell University for having provided me with financial aid for the duration of my studies, and Bar-Ilan University, for having assisted me with typing costs.

Finally, I wish to thank my loving wife and my dear parents whose unfailing love, devotion, counsel, and encouragement made it all possible.

שההחינו וקימנו והגיענו לזמן הזה.

Eugene J. Weinraub
Bar-Ilan University
Ramat-Gan, Israel
March, 1975

TABLE OF CONTENTS

	Page
INTRODUCTION	15

CHAPTER

		Page
I.	THE THEORY OF CHRISTIAN ORIGIN	21
II.	THE THEORY OF CELTIC ORIGIN	33
III.	A NEW JUDAIC INTERPRETATION	50
	Part One: The Seder as a model for Chrétien's Grail episode.	51
	The Questions and the Grail	55
	The Bleeding Lance	62
	The Candelabras	66
	The Meal	68
	Part Two: Contact between the Jews of Spain and France and relations between Jew and Christian in Northern France	78
IV.	THE DEVELOPMENT OF PERCEVAL	88
V.	INTERPRETATION AND CONCLUSIONS	102
BIBLIOGRAPHY		118
TABLE OF PLATES		132

TRANSLITERATION

א is not transliterated	ו = v (where not a vowel)	ל = l	פ = ph
ב = b	ז = z	מ = m	צ = tz
ב = v	ח = ḥ	נ = n	ק = k
ג,ג = g	ט = t	ס = s	ר = r
ד,ד = d	י = y	ע is not transliterated	שׁ = sh
ה = h	כ = k		שׂ = s
	כ = kh	פ = p	ת,ת = t

◌ָ = a	◌ֵ = e		
◌ָ = a	◌ִ = i		
◌ֹ, וֹ = o	◌ֶ = e		
◌ֻ, וּ = u	◌ֶ = e		vocal *sheva* = e
short ◌ָ = o	◌ָ = o		silent *sheva* is not transliterated
◌ֵי = ei	◌ֲ = a		

PLATE 2. Family *Seder* Scene. *The Sarajevo Haggadah*, Spanish, 14th Century.

INTRODUCTION

Despite Manessier's exhortation regarding its irretrievability,[1] the Grail has continued for over seven hundred years to capture the imaginations of a veritable army of knights, writers and scholars who joined in its quest. The first among them to compose a romance about this mysterious object (though admittedly the question of possible anterior sources does remain an open one), was Chrétien de Troyes (1135?-1191?).[2] However, because this author described the Grail in a most nebulous manner, a plethora of theories were advanced to explain its origin and nature, thus creating one of the fiercest and most intriguing literary battles of all times.

---

[1] *Perceval le Gallois ou le Conte du Graal publié d'après les manuscrits originaux*, ed. Ch[arles] Potvin (Mons, 1871), VI, vv. 45361-45362:
>Ne jà mais nus hom qui soit nés
>Nel vera si apiertement.

[2] Despite attempts to establish an exact chronology for Chrétien de Troyes's life and work, nothing certain is known about the dates of composition of Chrétien's works. All that is known of his biography has been gleaned from his writings, and is therefore hypothetical in nature. Since Chrétien's unfinished romance *Perceval* was dedicated to Philippe de Flandre (Philippe d'Alsace) who died in 1191, Chrétien must have begun his *Perceval* no later than that date. For a fuller discussion of the difficulties involved in establishing a chronology for Chrétien, see James Douglas Bruce, *The Evolution of Arthurian Romance from the Beginnings Down to the Year 1300* (Göttingen, 1923), I, 219-223; Anthime Fourrier, "Encore la chronologie des œuvres de Chrétien de Troyes," *Bulletin bibliographique de la Société Internationale Arthurienne*, II (1950), 69-88; Jean Misrahi, "New Light on the Chronology of Chrétien de Troyes?," *Bulletin bibliographique de la Société Internationale Arthurienne*, XI (1959), 89-120, and Paul Zumthor, "Toujours à propos de la date du *Conte del Graal*," *Le Moyen Age*, LXV, 4th Series, XIV (1959), 579-586.

For some, such as Jessie Weston, the sources and symbolism of the Grail are to be found in fertility rites.[3] For others, the Grail is strictly Christian, or liturgical in nature,[4] while for still others this enigmatic object is of purely Celtic origin.[5] Combinations of the latter two theories have been proposed,[6] and several lesser-known theories such as Pauphilet's "lost resurrection" thesis[7] and Holmes' "Judeo-Christian" hypothesis,[8] have been formulated in an effort to further clarify the significance of the Grail. The fact that no one theory (notwithstanding the ardent claims of its adherents) is, by itself, capable of untangling *all* the strands of the Grail story's intricate web, should

---

[3] See for example, *The Legend of Sir Perceval: Studies upon its Origin, Development and Position in the Arthurian Cycle*, 2 vols. (London, 1906-1909) and *From Ritual to Romance* (Cambridge, England, 1920).

[4] See for example, Rose J. Peebles, *The Legend of Longinus and its Connection with the Grail* (Baltimore, 1911); James Douglas Bruce, *The Evolution of Arthurian Romance from the Beginnings Down to the Year 1300* (Göttingen, 1923), I, pp. 219-268 (cf. 2nd ed., 1928); Eugène Anitchkof, "Le Saint Graal et les rites eucharistiques," *Romania*, LV (1929), 174-194; and Konrad Burdach, *Der Gral: Forschungen über seinen Ursprung und seinen Zusammenhang mit der Longinuslegende*, Forschungen zur Kirchen-und Geistesgeschichte, XIV (Stuttgart, 1938), pp. xviii-580.

[5] See for example, Arthur C. L. Brown, *The Origin of the Grail Legend* (Cambridge, Mass., 1943); Helaine Newstead, *Bran the Blessed in Arthurian Romance* (New York, 1939); Roger Sherman Loomis, *Arthurian Tradition and Chrétien de Troyes* (New York, 1949), pp. 333-459, and *Perceval, or the Story of the Grail by Chrétien de Troyes*, trans. Roger Sherman Loomis and Laura Hibbard Loomis in *Medieval Romances* (New York, 1957), pp. 3-7; J. Vendryès, "Les Eléments celtiques de la légende du Graal," *Etudes Celtiques*, V (1949), 1-50; Jean Marx, *La Légende arthurienne et le Graal* (Paris, 1952); Jean Frappier, *Chrétien de Troyes: L'Homme et l'œuvre*, Connaissance des Lettres, No. 50 (Paris, 1957), pp. 8-65, and 170-243.

[6] Frappier, *Le Roman breton: Perceval ou le Conte du Graal*, "Les Cours de Sorbonne" (Paris, 1966), pp. 85 and 104-105; hereafter cited as *Perceval; Chrétien de Troyes*, pp. 203-209); also William A. Nitze, "Le Bruiden, le château du Graal, et la lance-qui-saigne," *Les Romans du Graal aux XII° et XIII° siècles*, Colloques Internationaux du Centre National de la Recherche Scientifique, III, Strasbourg, 29 mars - 3 avril 1954 (Paris, 1956), pp. 279-295.

[7] Albert Pauphilet, *Le Legs du Moyen Age* (Melun, 1950), pp. 173-178, and "Au sujet du Graal," *Romania*, LXVI (1940-1941), 289-321, 481-504.

[8] Urban T. Holmes, Jr., *A New Interpretation of Chrétien's Conte del Graal*. University of North Carolina Studies in the Romance Languages and Literatures, No. 8 (Chapel Hill, 1948), and Urban T. Holmes, Jr. and Sister M. Amelia Klenke, O.P., *Chrétien, Troyes and the Grail* (Chapel Hill, 1959). Cf. Urban T. Holmes, Jr., *Chrétien de Troyes* (New York, 1970), pp. 22-23, 53, 153-167.

indicate that several different influences were at play in the making of this fascinating legend. It is therefore undoubtedly more advisable, when evaluating the merits of any one given theory, to do so in relative rather than in absolute terms.

Chrétien de Troyes, in his unfinished romance *Perceval*, describes the knightly, religious, and personal education of a young man. It is a captivating, endearing, and at times even comic tale of a very coarse, but highly intelligent Welsh lad who rejects the isolation imposed upon him by his mother to seek his vocation as a knight. In the process he learns to think for himself, to feel for, and to appreciate other human beings. He then becomes aware of his true identity and fully understands the meaning of the Passion.

The most important episode of this romance is the youth's visit to the Fisher King's castle. In this scene, young Perceval, who has already achieved the physical prowess and skill of a knight, but who is still lacking in the judgment and consideration commensurate with such a position, enters a castle to seek shelter. He is escorted to a hall where he sees a handsome, grey-haired nobleman sitting on a couch by a fire, reclining on his elbow. The gentleman who explains that he is physically unable to rise in greeting, invites his young visitor to sit at his side. He then asks his guest from what direction he has come and comments on the great distance of the youth's journey. Soon afterwards the kindly nobleman presents the young man with a sword brought in by a squire (2976-3184). [9]

As the two are conversing, a squire enters carrying a white lance from which a drop of blood flows. Perceval observes this unusual occurrence, but recalling the advice a lord had once offered him,

---

[9] Unless otherwise indicated, all references are to Chrétien de Troyes, *Le Roman de Perceval ou le Conte du Graal*, ed. William Roach, 2nd. ed., Textes Littéraires Français, No. 71 (Geneva, 1959). I have compared the critical passages of this edition with the corresponding passages of *Perceval le Gallois ou le Conte du Graal publié d'après les manuscrits originaux*, Pt. II, Vol. I, *Le Poème de Chrétien de Troyes et de ses continuateurs d'après le manuscrit de Mons*, ed. Charles Potvin (Mons, 1865). In the latter manuscript the second damsel holds a *taule ensement* (4409) instead of a *tailleoir d'argent* (cited as a variant). The fact that this manuscript later mentions *le tailleoir d'argent* (4465) should indicate that the reading of v. 4409 is incorrect. There are no further discrepancies of *any importance* among these two editions. There are likewise no major discrepancies between Roach's text and Hilka's (*Christian von Troyes sämtliche erhaltene Werke*, Vol. V: *Der Percevalroman [Li Contes del Graal]*, ed. Alfons Hilka [Halle, 1932]).

against talking too much, refrains from asking his host the meaning of this marvel. Two squires then enter, bearing golden candelabras. They are followed by a beautiful, well-dressed damsel holding between her hands a grail of fine gold, set with the most precious stones. She, in turn, is followed by a second maiden carrying a silver carving platter. Like the lance-bearer, the two damsels pass before the seated men and proceed into another chamber. Remembering the lord's caveat, Perceval again restrains himself from asking who is served with the grail. The master of the castle calls for water, and the two wash. A table is brought in, and a pure white cloth is laid upon it. They then partake of a sumptuous repast, the first course of which is a haunch of peppered venison carved on the silver platter and served upon a type of flat, round cake (3185-3289).

The wine, grape juice, and food at this meal were both copious and excellent. On several occasions during the dinner, Perceval notices the grail passing before him, but each time the youth refrains from asking his host who is served with it. Instead, he decides that he will find out from one of the squires the following day. After a dessert of exotic fruits, and draughts of different types of wines, both the host and his young guest go to bed. But when Perceval awakes the following morning, not a soul is to be seen in the castle. The youth finds his horse saddled. Mounting it, he rides through the gate and across the drawbridge, jumping clear of the bridge just as it begins to rise mysteriously beneath his horse's feet. He calls out, but no one answers his painful shouts (3290-3421).

This, in essence, is the Grail episode as described by Chrétien de Troyes. However, four times during the course of the romance, the author of *Le Conte du Graal* refers back to this scene, adding more information about it on each occasion. Soon after leaving the Grail Castle, Perceval meets his cousin who rebukes him severely for not having asked his host, the Fisher King, why the lance bled, and where the people carrying the objects were going. She informs him that, had he only asked these questions, the maimed king would have been cured and would be able to rule his land with beneficent results. Now much misery must befall the youth and others. She further states that all this is a consequence of Perceval's sin against his mother (i.e., his having deserted her) which caused her to die of grief for him (3466-3631).

At a later date, when Perceval is in Caerleon, at King Arthur's court, a loathly damsel arrives and similarly scolds the knight for having kept silent in the presence of the lance and the grail. She, too, describes the salutary effects Perceval's questions would have had upon the king and his land and explains that, because the king is now unable to rule, ladies will lose their husbands, lands will be laid waste, helpless maidens will remain orphans and many knights will die. In response to these harsh words, Perceval swears that he will devote his life to learning the identity of the person served with the grail, to finding the lance that bleeds, and to discovering the true reason for this phenomenon (4603-4740). Similarly, the chivalrous knight Gauvain, in a secondary and parallel plot, promises his contender, Guigambresil, that he will spend a year searching for the lance whose point sheds tears of blood and which was destined to destroy the entire kingdom of Logres (6088-6216).

In a final scene, Chrétien de Troyes unveils still more of the mystery which shrouds the Grail episode. Perceval, now penitent for having abandoned God and done "nothing but evil" for five years, confesses to a hermit on Holy Friday. He tells the saintly man that the cause of his iniquitous behavior was his failure to ask the Fisher King about the lance and the grail. But the hermit informs him that the true reason for his misery was the sin he had committed against his mother. It was this sin which prevented him from asking his host the appropriate questions. The hermit then explains that the Fisher King was the son of the man served with the grail. But this man, who was also the brother of both Perceval's mother and the hermit (and a king in his own right), was not served pike, lamprey or salmon with the grail. Rather, for twelve years he sustained himself with a single Mass wafer which was brought to him on it. "So sacred a thing is the grail, and he himself is so spiritual." The hermit then shows Perceval how to atone for his sins. The knight remains two days with the holy man, and receives communion on Easter Sunday (6217-6513). [10]

---

[10] I am assuming a unity of authorship for the hermitage scene and for the preceding Perceval episodes. Though some scholars have postulated the duality of *Le Conte du Graal* (e.g., M. de Riquer, "Perceval y Gauvain en 'Li contes del Graal,' " *Filologia Romanza*, IV [1957], 119-147, "La composición de 'Li contes del Graal,' " *Boletín de la Real Academia de Buenas Letras de Barcelona*, XXVII [1957-1958], 279-320; Ph. Aug. Becker,

This then, in summary form, is Chrétien de Troyes's Grail episode — a few pages of text which have caused countless pages of interpretation to be written. It is to these that we now turn.

In the following pages I should like to advance a new theory for the origin of Chrétien's Grail scene. While both the Christian and Celtic interpretations (the two major Grail theories) do explain a certain number of the details found in Chrétien de Troyes's *Perceval*, I believe that the interpretation I am about to offer will have the dual advantage of explaining a larger number of these details while at the same time being based upon a highly compressed and completely organic source; namely, a religious ritual practiced annually by Jewish families for over three thousand years. In partial support of my theory, I shall refer to medieval Hebraic textual and iconographic descriptions of this rite, many of these being composed by residents of Troyes or by travelers who had visited that city, who were the contemporaries of our author. I shall then attempt to demonstrate that it would have been highly possible for a resident of twelfth-century Troyes to have been either directly or indirectly acquainted with this most widespread Jewish custom.

But inasmuch as the Grail episode is part of a larger work, we must return to the *Conte du Graal* to examine how this episode fits into the general framework of this romance and then ask ourselves how the Judaic origin of such a scene would effect the interpretation of the work as a whole.

However, before proceeding with a new interpretation of Chrétien's Grail scene, we shall do well to critically examine the two classical Grail theories so that we may approach the problem from a better perspective.

"Von den Erzählern neben und nach Chrestien de Troyes," *Zeitschrift für romanische Philologie*, LV [1935], 385-445; D. D. R. Owen, *The Evolution of the Grail Legend* [Edinburgh, 1968]; Leo Pollmann, *Chrétien de Troyes und der 'Conte del Graal'* [Tübingen, 1965]), the arguments for the unity of the work presented by such scholars as J. Frappier ("Note complémentaire sur la composition du 'Conte du Graal,'" *Romania*, LXXXI [1960], 308-337) and E. Köhler ("Zur Diskussion über die Einheit von Chrestiens 'Li Conte del Graal,'" *Zeitschrift für romanische Philologie*, LXXXIX [1959], 523-539) seem to me more convincing. I shall mention some of the arguments for the unity of *Le Conte du Graal* in the next chapter.

In this study I shall concentrate on the Perceval episodes of *Le Conte du Graal*.

PLATE 3. *Above Left:* Ha Laḥma Anya, "This is the Bread of Affliction." *The Sarajevo Haggadah*, 14th Century, Spanish.
Above Right: Samaritan Paschal Sacrifice.
Below: The Passover Sacrifice depicted on a *Seder* Plate.

PLATE 4. *Above:* Perforating Designs upon the *Matzot*. *Haggadah* MS, Münich Museum, 15th Century.
Below: Haggadah Fragments and *Seder* Illustrations on a *Seder* Plate.

Chapter I

THE THEORY OF CHRISTIAN ORIGIN

The proponents of the Christian theory begin their argument by claiming that the general framework of Chrétien de Troyes's writing is religious in nature and that the author of *Le Conte du Graal* amplified such pietistic elements in this, his final work.[1] They cite as proof the abundance of religious formulae and gestures, the prayers and the descriptions of the Passion found in *Perceval*. Though the theory of Christian origin contains numerous variants, they all may be classified under one of two rubrics. According to the "Christian theorist" whom one consults, the procession at the Fisher King's castle would represent either: a Roman mass, or rather, a communion administered to a moribund person; or a liturgical ceremony of the Byzantine church.

Some "communionists" believe that the grail, containing a host (which might have been unconsecrated) represents a ciborium, a chalice, or a symbolic combination of both these articles. The words *trestot descovert* which Chrétien uses to describe the grail (v. 3301) refer then, to an "unveiled chalice."[2] In a like manner the carving platter would symbolize a paten, and the bleeding lance would be the Holy Lance of Longinus (the traditional name of the blind Roman

---

[1] See for example, Paul Imbs, "L'Elément religieux dans le Conte del Graal de Chrétien de Troyes," *Les Romans du Graal*, pp. 31-53, esp. pp. 44-48.
[2] A. Hilka (*Perceval ou Li Contes del Graal*, pp. 687-688) interprets verse 3301 in this manner. M. Lot-Borodine ("Autour du Saint Graal," *Romania*, LVII [1931], 185-186) shares this interpretation.

centurion who pierced the side of the crucified Jesus with his spear and who was cured of his blindness by a drop of blood which issued forth from the wound).[3]

Others, as for example Prof. Imbs, taking into account both the verses:

> "Mais ne quidiez pas que il ait
> Lus ne lamproie ne salmon;
> D'une sole oiste le sert on,
> Que l'en en cel graal li porte;
> Sa vie sostient et conforte,
> Tant sainte chose est li graals" (6420-6425)

and Hélinand de Froidmont's famous thirteenth-century definition of a grail:

> Gradalis autem sive gradale Gallice dicitur scutella lata, et aliquantulum profunda; in qua pretiosae dapes cum suo jure divitibus solent apponi gradatim, unus morsellus post alium in diversis ordinibus; et dicitur vulgari nomine *graalz*, quia grata et acceptabilis est in ea comedenti: tum propter continens, quia forte argentea est, vel alia pretiosa materia; tum propter contentum, id est ordinem multiplicem pretiosarum dapum.[4]

claim that Chrétien's grail must have been a plate, greater in width than in depth, large enough to contain a pike, lamprey or salmon. Prof. Imbs, by an analysis of Chrétien's use of the word *saint*, arrives at the conclusion that the expression *tant sainte chose* must refer to the *Paropsis*, Jesus' plate at the Last Supper.[5] According to Robert de Boron's poem (*Le Roman de l'Estoire du Graal*, beginning of the 13th century, no later than 1215)[6] — but not according to Chrétien's —

---

[3] John 19:34: "One of the soldiers pierced his side with a lance; and immediately there came out blood and water." *The Jerusalem Bible*, ed. Alexander Jones (Garden City, New York, 1966), p. 188. Unless otherwise indicated, all references are to this edition.

[4] Helinandus Frigidi Montis Monachis, *Chronicon.*—Lib. XLV. An. 720, Migne, *Patrologiae Series Latina*, CCXII, Cols. 814-815. Cf. Frappier, *Chrétien de Troyes*, p. 188, *Perceval*, p. 5.

[5] Matthew 26:23: "He answered, "Someone who has dipped his hand into the dish with me will betray me," p. 58. See Imbs, "L'Elément religieux," *Les Romans du Graal*, p. 44.

[6] Chronology of Frappier, *Perceval*, p. 9. The dating of Robert de Boron's work is subject to as much debate as that of Chrétien's. Eugène Anitchkof (*Romania* [LV], p. 176) questions the traditional chronology

Joseph of Arimathaea had collected Jesus' blood in this relic of the Passion which was none other than our grail.[7]

In response to those who find it difficult to believe that Chrétien's grail, carried by a woman, could be a ciborium or a chalice with which only a *priest* is allowed to administer communion, scholars such as Alfons Hilka claim that in an emergency situation a woman is permitted to administer communion to a moribund person.[8] They cite the writings of ecclesiastical figures such as Giraldus Cambrensis (a contemporary of Chrétien) as testimony to the prevalence of Holy Communion administered in this manner.[9] Chrétien's Grail episode would then be a representation of such a communion. A. Micha, in a related, but somewhat unconvincing interpretation, maintains that Chrétien de Troyes transformed the ceremonial cross of a eucharistic procession into a bleeding lance, and that similarly, the other participants in his Grail procession, lost their original clerical form.[10]

Before examining the merits of the Roman Mass theory, let us look at the second manifestation of the theory of Christian origin—

---

which places Chrétien's *Perceval* before the *Roman du Saint Graal* of Robert de Boron. James D. Bruce, in a discussion of the matter (*The Evolution of Arthurian Romance* I, 219-223) allows for the possibility that Robert de Boron's *Joseph (Le Roman de l'Estoire du Graal)* preceded Chrétien's *Perceval*, though he believes it unlikely.

[7] Imbs, "L'Elément religieux," *Les Romans du Graal*, pp. 38-44.

[8] Dass (in Vertretung eines Priesters) eine Jungfrau diesen Hostienbehälter ans Lager des alten Mannes bringen darf, weicht gewiss von kirchlichen Vorschriften ab, ist aber nicht ganz unbezeugt. (*Christian von Troyes sämtliche erhaltene Werke*, Vol. V: *Der Percevalroman* [*Li Contes del Graal*], ed. Alfons Hilka [Halle, 1932], p. 682, v. 3221n.)

[9] Giraldus Cambrensis, "Gemma Ecclesiastica," ed. J. S. Brewer, *Opera* (London, 1862), II, 13: Item in eadem distinctione ex concilio Remensi "Pervenit ad notitiam nostram quod quidam presbyteri in tantum parvipendant divina misteria ut laico aut foeminae sacrum corpus Domini tradant ad deferendum infirmis, et quibus prohibetur ne sacrarium ingrediantur, nec ad altare appropinquant, illis sancta sanctorum committuntur, quod quam sit horribile quamque detestabile omnium religiosorum animadvertit prudentia. Igitur interdicit per omnia synodus ne talis temeraria praesumtio ulterius fiat; sed omnimodo presbyter per semetipsum infirmum communicet; quod si fecerit aliter gradus sui periculo subjacebit."

Portions of this text and texts appearing on pp. 14, 29, 31 and 36 of the above work are cited by Hilka (*ibid.*) as "proof" that such communions did take place. Cf. the list of texts furnished by A. Micha in his remarks on Prof. Loomis' paper (*Les Romans du Graal*, p. 247) which show the frequency of this forbidden practice at the time of Chrétien de Troyes.

[10] "Deux études sur le graal, I: Le Graal et la Lance," *Romania*, LXXIII (1952), 473.

the Byzantine thesis. This interpretation sees Chrétien's Grail procession as a representation of the Grand Entrance (*megale episodos*) ceremony of the Mass of St. John Chrysostom. In this ritual, the officiants first prepare the Holy Species in a portion of the sanctuary separated by a screen from the worshippers. They then enter the main part of the church in procession, bearing lighted candles, the *diskos* ("paten" — a round, slightly cupped plate upon which rest the portions of bread to be consecrated), the chalice, the *hagia longkhe* (a knife with a triangular blade, which represents the Holy Lance and which the priest had just used to "wound" the eucharist symbolically), as well as a crucifix, a sponge, fans, evangeliaria, reliquaries, church banners, and the bishop's pallium. According to this thesis, Chrétien's grail would, of course, be the *diskos,* and his bleeding lance the *hagia longkhe.* [11] Just as this rite emphasizes the *diskos* by placing it before the lance, so did Chrétien accent the grail by including it in the title of his romance. [12]

Here then are both forms of the theory of Christian origin. However, its defenders are pitted against a powerful, well-organized opposition, quick to discover and to attack the theory's numerous weak points. The Christian thesis, first of all, presupposes a functional relationship between the description of the grail at the hermitage and Chrétien's previous references to this object. But as many opponents observe, this basic assumption may not necessarily be valid. They note that only in the hermitage episode does the grail assume a reli-

---

[11] See Anitchkof, *Romania,* LV (1929), 182-194, esp. 191-193; Bruce, *Evolution of Arthurian Romance,* I, 257-259; Konrad Burdach, *Der Gral* (Stuttgart, 1938), pp. 130-150, "Zum Ursprung der Salomo-Sage," *Archiv für das Studium der neueren Sprachen,* CVIII (1902), 121-132, "Theologie und Kirchenwesen," *Deutsche Literaturzeitung,* XXIV (1902), cols. 3050-3058; Frappier, *Perceval,* p. 85; Richard Heinzel, *Ueber di französischen Gralromane,* Denkschriften der Kaiserlichen Akademie der Wissenschaften, *Philolosophisch-historische Classe,* XL, pt. 3 (Vienna, 1892); Myrrha Lot-Borodine, "Autour du saint Graal: A propos de travaux récents," *Romania,* LVII (1931), 147-205; Jean Marx, *La Légende arthurienne et le Graal* (Paris, 1952), pp. 235-240; also Paulus Cassel, *Der Gral und sein Name,* 2nd ed. (Berlin, 1878), p. 10; C. A. Swainson, *The Greek Liturgies* (Cambridge, England, 1884), 101 ff. esp. 104 ff.; and J. M. Neale, *History of the Eastern Church* (London, 1850), I, 342, cited by Bruce, *The Evolution of Arthurian Romance,* I, pp. 257-258.

[12] Nitze, "Le Bruiden," *Les Romans du Graal,* p. 292.

gious character. Nothing in Chrétien's previous references to this object suggests that the grail possessed a sacramental nature. Even Chrétien's use of the word *merveille* (v. 3202) in connection with the bleeding lance does not imply a religious significance, since Chrétien only once associates this word with a miracle (*Cligès*, v. 2732) and then only figuratively, in the sense of an astonishing phenomenon. In all other places (e.g. *Yvain*, v. 1202 and *Le Conte du Graal*, v. 7826) the word is synonymous with enchantment. These opponents thus conclude that Chrétien was not the author of the Good Friday episode.[13]

To be fair, we must note that Professor Imbs is able to parry this attack rather effectively. According to him, Chrétien, in his description of the Fisher King's castle, made no allusion to the religious nature of the grail because he was presenting the scene as viewed through Perceval's eyes. Furthermore the author may have intentionally desired to save the religious character of his story for the end in order to heighten the suspense of his narrative.

Similarly the objections raised by certain critics against the presumed relationship between the lance and the grail (i.e., the lance seems somewhat subordinate to the grail: the grail alone is found in the title of the romance, the lance appears only once in the procession, and it alone is sought by Gauvain) may be, if not completely overruled, at least greatly weakened by the replies of Professors Imbs and Hofer:

> Il reste que la *lance et le Graal sont à peu près constamment associés* lorsque Chrétien *rappelle les questions que Perceval devait poser.* ... Si ... Chrétien ne dit pas que la lance repasse avec le Graal c'est par *brachylogie*: Chrétien ne nomme que le plus important des deux objets. ... Si Gauvain part à la recherche de la lance, sa mission n'est pas la même que celle de *Perceval*.[14]

However, much more serious objections confront the defenders of the Christian theses. First, none of these theories is all-inclusive; none

---

[13] See Imbs, "L'Elément religieux," *Les Romans du Graal*, pp. 38 and 49.

[14] *Ibid.*, p. 50. Stefan Hofer similarly sees a close association between the lance and grail though he believes the lance is given a superior position in Chrétien's romance (*Chrétien de Troyes: Leben und Werke des altfranzösischen Epikers* [Graz-Köln, 1954], pp. 206-207).

can explain, for example, the matter of the unasked questions. As we know, Perceval's questions play a capital role in the romance. In the Grail scene itself, Chrétien repeatedly reminds his reader of Perceval's failure to ask the appropriate questions:

> Li vallés voit cele merveille [the bleeding lance]
> Qui la nuit ert laiens venus,
> Se s'est de demander tenus
> Comment ceste chose avenoit,
> ... ...
> Et li vallés les vit passer,
> Ne n'osa mie demander
> Del graal cui l'en en servoit. (3202-3205, 3243-3245)

The author underlines this fact by abandoning his neutrality to voice his apprehension regarding the sagacity of Perceval's behavior:

> Si criem que il n'i ait damage,
> Por che que j'ai oi retraire
> Qu'ausi se puet on bien trop taire
> Com trop parler a la foie[e].
> Ou biens l'en viegne ou mals l'en chiee,
> Ne sai le quel rien n'en demande. (3248-3253)

Like a matador in the arena, Chrétien passes the grail before the eyes of young Perceval in an effort to incite him to ask about it:

> Et li graals endementiers
> Par devant als retrespassa,
> Ne li vallés ne demanda
> Del graal cui on en servoit. (3290-3293)

And as if the reader were still unaware of the importance of these questions, Chrétien repeats his commentary a second time:

> *Mais plus se taist qu'il ne covient,*
> Qu'a chascun mes que l'on servoit,
> Par devant lui trespasser voit
> Le graal trestot descovert,
> Ne ne set pas cui l'en en sert
> Et si le volroit il savoir.
> Mais il le demandera voir,
> Ce dist et pense, ains qu'il s'en tort,
> A un des vallés de la cort;

> Mais jusqu'al matin atendra,
> Que al seignor congié prendra
> Et a toute l'autre maisnie.
> Einsi la chose a respitie. (3298-3311)[15]

On the morrow Perceval once again hopes to learn the answers to his questions from the squires:

> Savoir se nus d'als li diroit
> De la lance por qu'ele saine,
> Se il puet estre en nule paine,
> Et del graal ou l'en le porte; (3398-3401)

and on leaving the castle he makes one last, desperate attempt to discover the answers by asking the mysterious person who raised the drawbridge:

> "Di va! ... tu qui le pont
> As levé, cor parole a moi.
> Ou iex tu quant je ne te voi?
> Trai toi avant, si te verrai
> Et d'autre chose t'enquerrai
> Noveles que savoir voldroie." (3414-3419)

Three times Perceval's cousin rebukes him for not having asked his host the proper questions (3554-3555, 3571 and 3583-3592), and at King Arthur's court the Loathly Damsel does the same. According to her, it was Perceval's *silence* which caused the Fisher King's land to forfeit its chances for peace:

> "A mal eür tu [te] teüsses,
> Que se tu demandé l'eüsses,
> Li riches rois, qui or s'esmaie,
> Fust ja toz garis de sa plaie
> Et si tenist sa terre en pais,
> Dont il ne tendra point jamais.
> ... ...
> Dames en perdront lor maris,
> Terres en seront escillies
> Et puceles desconseillies,

---

[15] Italics mine.

> Qui orfenines remandront,
> Et maint chevalier en morront;
> Tot cist mal esteront par toi." (4669-4674),
> 4678-4683)

Finally Perceval, confessing to the hermit, tells the saintly man that the source of his sin was his failure to have questioned his host:

> "... rien n'en demandai.
> ... ...
> Si ai puis eü si grant doel
> Que mors eüsse esté mon wel." (6377, 6381-6382)

Yet although it is more than obvious that Chrétien intended to stress the theme of these unasked questions, none of the two Christian theories has a word to say about them; nor do they explain how Perceval's having asked the questions would effect the Fisher King's cure and re-establish his realm.

Still other weaknesses impair the effectiveness of the Christian theses. Frappier notes that though the communion of a moribund person explains, or seems to explain the presence of a female Grail Bearer, it cannot explain the presence of a lance. Similarly, the Byzantine hypothesis, which appears to explain the presence of a lance is unable to explain the presence of a female Grail Bearer.[16] In order to overcome these difficulties, certain Christian theorists thought of combining the two theories into one, but Frappier summarily dismisses their efforts with the words "Et l'on semble trouver tout naturel que pour imaginer la scène du cortège Chrétien de Troyes ait eu besoin de penser *à la fois* à une forme insolite de la communion des malades et au rite exotique de la Grande Entrée byzantine."[17]

But we may carry our attack still further. If the grail and the carving platter represent a ciborium and a paten respectively, why is Chrétien's grail made of gold and his carving platter of silver,[18] inas-

---

[16] Frappier, *Perceval*, p. 85.
[17] *Ibid.* Cf. Frappier, "Le 'Conte du Graal' est-il une allégorie judéo-chrétienne? (II)," *Romance Philology*, XX (1966), 12.
[18]
> Aprés celi en revint une
> Qui tint un tailleoir d'argant.
> Li graaus, qui aloit devant,
> De fin or esmeré estoit;
> Prescïeuses pierres avoit

much as the canonical rule states that the paten must be of the same metal as the ciborium? [19] Moreover, if Chrétien's grail is already carrying a host, why the need for a paten (carving platter)? And if the carving platter is indeed a paten, Chrétien, would have a squire carve a haunch of peppered venison on this sacred article — a practice which is clearly inadmissible:

> De la hance de cerf al poivre
> Uns valles devant als trencha,
> Qui a lui traite la hanche a
> Atot *le tailleoir d'argant,*
> Et les morsiax lor met devant
> Sor un gastel qui fu entiers. (3284-3289) [20]

Moreover, according to Frappier, the word *tailleoir* belonged (as did *graal*) to a culinary vocabulary, signifying a plate or platter upon which meat was carved. [21] Such a receptacle would seem definitely

---

> El graal de maintes manieres,
> Des plus riches et des plus chieres
> Qui en mer ne en terre soient (3230-3237).

[19] Lot-Borodine, "Autour du Saint Graal," *Romania*, LVII (1931), 189; Cf. Frappier, *Perceval*, p. 86; and Pietro Siffrin, "Patena," *Enciclopedia Cattolica*: "Patena è un piatto rotundo di metallo usato già anticamente nalla Messa come complemento indespensabile del calice e fatto dello stesso metallo." We should note that for Sister M. Amelia Klenke the interpretation of the canonical text cited above by Mrs. Lot-Borodine is different. According to Sister Amelia (*Chrétien, Troyes, and the Grail*, p. 172), "... different metals are admissible together today just as in the twelfth century (see my 'Liturgy and Allegory in Chrétien's Perceval,' p. 13)." But the case which Sister Amelia cites (*Liturgy and Allegory in Chrétien's Perceval*, University of North Carolina Studies in the Romance Lang. and Lit., XIV [Chapel Hill, 1951], p. 13) of Saint-Exupère's having administered communion with a glass and wicker basket (not a paten made of reeds as Sister Amelia seems to imply) appears to have been a highly irregular procedure. It was because he had sold the church's vessels to help the poor that he had to "improvise" with commonly available utensils (see H. Leclerq, "Calice," *Dictionnaire d'archéologie chrétienne et de la liturgie* [Paris, 1910], II, col. 608). In all other examples cited by Leclerq the chalice and paten are made of the *same* material. Cf., M. Trens' description of medieval metallic chalices and patens (*La Eucaristía en el Arte español* [Barcelona, 1952], pp. 271-283). Even if there were no conclusive evidence that the paten and chalice *had* to be constructed of the same material, it would be logical to assume that in most cases they were, since they were used together as a "set." This in the very least would reduce the probability that Chrétien's grail and carving platter were a chalice and paten.

[20] Italics mine.

[21] "Le 'Conte du Graal' est-il une allégorie judéo-chrétienne? (II)," p. 17.

out of place in a eucharistic procession. Finally, Professors Loomis and Frappier ask, if the Grail procession were in effect a mass, why does no one cross himself or genuflect? [22]

If on the one hand we admit that the Grail scene describes the communion of a moribund person, how do we account for the fact that there is no dying person present? The hermit explicitly states that the person served by the grail is an ascetic, who is not at all in danger of death — Chrétien speaks of the nutritive powers of the host. Furthermore, as Frappier remarks, the liturgical theory is incapable of furnishing a plausible explanation for the repeated appearances of the grail. "Que signifierait en effet une communion de malade répétée de la sorte?" [23] Pursuing his criticism further, Frappier adds that the words *trestot descovert* do not refer to an unveiled chalice (as assumed by certain Christian theorists) but rather they simply mean *very apparent*. [24] Finally, as Frappier observes, neither the Loathly

---

[22] Frappier, *Perceval*, p. 86; Roger Sherman Loomis, "Les Légendes hagiographes et la légende du Graal," *Les Romans du Graal*, pp. 233-234. We should add that Professor Imbs, replying to Professor Loomis' challenge, claims that there was no one in the room who could have made such gestures. The Fisher King was wounded and incapable of any movement, while Perceval understood nothing of what was occurring (*Ibid.*, p. 246). However, it appears to me that Professor Imbs is overlooking the fact that there were servants present throughout the meal. The nobleman sent *deus serjans* to escort Perceval to him (3081-3082). During the entire Grail procession there were *vallés* behind Perceval and the young knight commanded the arms squire to hold his newly acquired sword for him (3180-3184). The movements of these servants were minutely recorded by Chrétien as they performed their table service during the meal (3254-3255, 3260-3261, 3266-3267, 3285, 3322-3323) and their domestic duties afterwards (3344-3345, 3350-3355). During the banquet Perceval remarks that he will ask one of the squires about the grail (3305-3307) the following day; and Chrétien states that the next day Perceval found no living being, neither a squire or servant (3384-3385), indicating again that such individuals were present the previous evening. It appears to me that if Chrétien had intended the Grail *cortège* to represent a eucharistic procession, he would only have been emphasizing the sacramental character of the objects if he had described religious gestures performed by the servants. It would furthermore seem highly surprising that he should fail to do so since he so carefully recorded the other activities of the servants.

[23] Frappier, *Perceval*, p. 95. We should note in passing that nowhere in the text does it say that each time the grail passes it serves someone.

[24] "Sur l'interprétation du vers 3301 du *Conte du Graal*: 'Le graal trestot descovert,'" *Romania*, LXXI (1950), 240-245; "Autres remarques sur le vers 3301 du *Conte du Graal*," *Bulletin bibliographique de la Société Interna-*

Damsel nor the hermit attach the slightest importance, nor make the slightest allusion to the Grail Maiden. "Elle s'évanouit sur les lèvres dans l'anonymat peu glorieux d'un 'on'." If the Grail banquet were an emergency communion of a moribund person, the presence of female eucharist bearers would surely be remarked. [25]

If on the other hand we admit the Byzantine hypothesis, we are hard-pressed to explain why Chrétien's scene takes place in a castle, during the course of a banquet rather than in a church, why there are no priests or deacons in the procession, why the order of the articles in the eucharistic procession should be changed, and why their number should be reduced to four. [26] Moreover, how can one equate the purely beneficent Holy Lance of Longinus, which not only cured the centurion but according to Saint Ambrose "lavat peccatum totius mundi," with Chrétien's bleeding lance, which (though beneficent to the Fisher King) is highly maleficent since it is destined to destroy the entire kingdom of Logres?

> Et s'est escrit qu'il ert une hore
> Que toz li roiames de Logres,
> Qui jadis fu la terre as ogres,
> Sera destruis par cele lance. (6168-6171)

Furthermore, since no text prior to Chrétien de Troyes ever credited the Holy Lance with bleeding, why then should Chrétien introduce this "romantic adaptation" (to use Professor Imbs' expression), into his text? Because of these difficulties Frappier believes Chrétien de Troyes must have found the prototype for his *lance-qui-saigne* elsewhere. [27]

---

tionale Arthurienne, II (1950), 89-93; and "Du 'Graal trestot descovert' à l'origine de la légende," *Romania*, LXXIV (1953), 358-375.

[25] "Le 'Conte du Graal' est-il une allégorie judéo-chrétienne? (II)," pp. 14-15.

[26] One may also wonder why the *hagia longkhe* — a knife, i.e., an object of reduced dimensions — is depicted by Chrétien as a lance (i.e., an object of larger size) that bleeds.

[27] See Laura Hibbard Loomis, "The Passion Lance Relic and the War Cry Monjoie in the Chanson de Roland and Related Texts," *Romanic Review*, XLI (1950), 241-260; Frappier, *Cours*, pp. 85-89; Imbs, "L'Elémént religieux," *Les Romans du Graal*, p. 51; "The Holy Grail," *Encyclopaedia Britannica* (Chicago, 1968), X, 659.

One final snare threatens the advocates of the Christian theses. These scholars experience great difficulty in explaining (or do not even attempt to explain) the personage of the maimed Fisher King.

Here then is the Christian hypothesis. To use (again) Professor Imbs' words, it does give "a certain coherency" to the Grail procession. However, if we attempt to uncover closer parallels between either the Roman or Byzantine masses and Chrétien's Grail episode we encounter a host of unresolvable difficulties.

PLATE 5. *Seder* Plate. Faience. Pesaro, Italy, 1614.

PLATE 6. *Seder* Plate. Majolica. Ancona, Italy, 1673.

CHAPTER II

THE THEORY OF CELTIC ORIGIN

If certain problems confront the "communionists" or liturgists, perhaps the "Celtologists" are more successful in explaining the Grail episode. Indeed according to their claims, the theory of Celtic origin respects the unity of Chrétien's story, and, unlike the Roman Mass theory, it does not separate the grail from the lance. To be sure, no one will deny the presence of a supernatural element in *Perceval* — even Professor Imbs will admit this.¹ But the defenders of the Celtic theory choose to interpret the entire Grail scene as directly attributable to Celtic sources. They believe that sufficient historical evidence exists to demonstrate that by the middle of the twelfth century there was already a widespread Arthurian tradition of Irish and Welsh origin in England and on the Continent.²

Seen through the eyes of these theorists, the grail would be one of the talismans of the Other World such as the ale cup in *The*

---

¹ Imbs, "L'Elément religieux," *Les Romans du Graal*, pp. 49-50.
² Stefan Hofer (*Chrétien de Troyes: Leben und Werke des altfranzösischen Epikers* [Graz-Köln, 1954], p. 37) summarizes their proof as follows: In addition to the testimony of William of Malmesbury, who was read in learned circles only, the Celtic theorists base their argument upon: Herman of Tournai's mention of King Arthur in 1113; sculptures on the portal of the Modena Cathedral (beginning of the twelfth century) bearing Arthurian names; documented proof of the existence of the names *Artusius* and *Galvanus* in northern Italy, between 1114 and 1136; Giraldus Cambrensis' references to the *cantatores Britonum* and the Fee *Morgain*; the troubadour Marcabrun's comparison of himself to Arthur in his lament upon the death of his patron William X of Poitou (died 1137); and mention of Arthur's palace in the 1120 *Liber floridus* of Lambert of Saint Omer.

Phantom's Frenzy (*Baile in Scáil*, eleventh century, Irish)[3] or the supernatural cups of *Kulhwch and Olwen* or *Branwen Daughter of Llyr* (Welsh, second half of the tenth and early in the second half of the eleventh centuries respectively).[4] Professor Nitze, remarks that "le caractère nourricier du Graal est un élément païen;"[5] and Frappier, observing that Chrétien stressed the nutritive power of the host which *sustained* and *comforted* the Fisher King's father for twelve years, believes that Chrétien may have substituted the grail for a Celtic cauldron — a magical recipient capable of dispensing food and drink according to one's desire.[6] Similarly the prototype of Chrétien's grail may have been an inexhaustible plate such as the *dysgl* of Rhydderch Hael[7] or the hamper of Gwyddneu Garanhir.[8] Frappier conjectures that Chrétien's juxtaposition of the grail's appearances with his descriptions of sumptuous fare *may* have been a hint on the part of the author that a causal relationship existed between the grail and the host.[9] In the paper he presented at the Grail colloquium of the C.N.R.S., he categorically states that the host was spontaneously generated by the grail, thus likening it to the Celtic talismans.[10] He accordingly interprets the verb *vient* ("Fors l'oiste qui el graal vient" [6428]) as synonymous with the verbs *croître* "to grow" and *pousser*, "to spring up."[11] Thus, he feels that Chrétien transformed, rationalized and Christianized certain elements of Celtic origin in composing his *Conte du Graal*.[12]

According to the Celtic interpretation, the bleeding lance would be an instrument similar to the one of the god Oengus, king of the

---

[3] Myles Dillon, *Early Irish Literature* (Chicago, 1948), pp. 107-109; cf. Arthur C. L. Brown, *The Origin of the Grail Legend* (Cambridge, Mass., 1943), pp. 218-220.

[4] Gwyn Jones and Thomas Jones, trans. *The Mabinogion* (London and New York, 1963), p. ix.

[5] "Discussion of Prof. Imb's Paper," *Les Romans du Graal*, p. 53.

[6] *Perceval*, p. 95.

[7] See Charlotte Guest, trans. *The Mabinogion* (London and Toronto, 1919), p. 328.

[8] Jones and Jones, *The Mabinogion*, p. 115; Guest, *The Mabinogion*, p. 114.

[9] *Perceval*, p. 95.

[10] "Sa présence [the presence of the host] est spontanée... elle ne dépend de rien d'autre que du plat" ("Le Graal et l'Hostie [*Conte del Graal*, v. 6413-6431]," *Les Romans du Graal*, pp. 66-67).

[11] *Ibid.*, pp. 63-78.

[12] *Perceval*, pp. 95-96.

spirit folk *Túatha Dé Danann.* [13] This god known as *Gaifhuilech* ("with the bloody lance") possessed a lance stained with blood, which he used to blind Cormac for having raped his sister. [14] Some Celtic theorists see Chrétien's lance as the lance of the god Lug or that of Kulhwch, which was capable of drawing blood from the wind; whereas the lance of Pisear (whose quest Lug imposed upon the sons of Tuirenn) or the *Luin* of Celtchar son of Uthider in *The Battle of Moytura* were also proposed as sources for the *lance-qui-saigne*. [15] Professor Jean Marx identifies these two weapons with the lance of Oengus and further believes that the Dolorous Stroke which had maimed the Fisher King was performed by this very lance. [16]

One of the advantages of the theory of Celtic origin is that it explains or seems to explain the presence of the Fisher King. According to some Celtic theorists, this personage would be the Irish god Nuadu, whose name means "fisher" and who corresponds to the British god Nodens. He is king of the *Túatha Dé Danann* and is credited with possessing a silver sword and a cauldron of abundance. In addition, he is wounded, and consequently unable to reign. [17] Other *celtisants* believe that the Fisher King was really the Welsh god Bran the Blessed, who was associated with the sea, who possessed a magic cauldron as well as a horn of plenty and who suffered from a lance wound in his foot which forced him to abandon his throne. [18]

Another important detail which the Celtic theory appears to explain is the matter of Perceval's questions. These would correspond

---

[13] Part of the Irish mythological cycle. See Dillon, *Early Irish Literature*, pp. 51-72.

[14] Marx, *La Légende arthurienne et le Graal*, p. 131.

[15] Junes and Jones, *The Mabinogion*, p. 122; cf. Frappier, *Perceval*, p. 97; and Thomas Parry, *A History of Welsh Literature*, trans. H. Idris Bell (Oxford, 1955), p. 79.

[16] Marx, *La Légende arthurienne et le Graal*, p. 257.

[17] See Frappier, *Perceval*, pp. 98-99, and *Chrétien de Troyes*, pp. 200-201; also Marx, *La Légende arthurienne et le Graal*, pp. 143-144. Professor Vendryès concurs that the Celtic god Nodens, called "the silver-handed" because he lost his hand in battle is Chrétien's Fisher King (*Les Romans du Graal*, p. 78).

[18] Helaine Newstead, *Bran the Blessed in Arthurian Romance* (New York, 1939), pp. 6, 11, 14, 15, 18-19, 23, 39, 67, 86-120. Incidentally, the related theme of the Wasteland is basic to Celtic literature, recurring in such tales as *Llud and Llefelys* in Wales (See Parry, *History of Welsh Literature*, p. 80), and the stories of *Lugaid MacNiad* and *Conaire Mor* in Ireland.

to the repeated question "To whom shall be given the beaker with the red beer?" which the beautiful Sovranty of Ireland asked the god Lug in *The Phantom's Frenzy*. Frappier remarks that both this text and Chrétien's *Perceval* contain the theme of the granting and reestablishment of sovereignty brought about by the asking of questions.[19] If Perceval was unable to ask the questions it was no doubt due to a *geis*, i.e., an interdiction, imposed upon him.

The advocates of the Celtic theory would view Chrétien's female Grail Bearer as one of the feminine figures of the Other World who carry such royal talismans as vases of plenty and sovereignty — a figure like the Sovranty of Ireland. This personage is often depicted as a hideous witch who demands either a kiss or the love of the hapless warrior who should chance upon her abode. In one text she is transformed into a radiant girl.[20] This transformation prompted Frappier to propose that the Loathly Damsel is none other than the Grail Bearer of the Fisher King's castle.[21]

Finally, according to the *celtisants*, the moat over which Perceval had to pass to enter and leave the Fisher King's castle[22] would be a remnant of the Irish legendary circumnavigations — *imrama*, and the Grail Castle itself would be a representation of the Celtic Other World.[23]

---

[19] *Perceval*, p. 102; see also Marx, *La Légende arthurienne et le Graal*, pp. 273-277; Dillon, *Early Irish Literature*, pp. 107-110; Roger Sherman Loomis, *The Grail: From Celtic Myth to Christian Symbol* (Cardiff and New York, 1963), pp. 47-53.

[20] Marx, *La Légende arthurienne et le Graal*, pp. 273-274.

[21] *Perceval*, p. 102.

[22] Einsi vers la porte s'en va;
Devant la porte un pont trova
Torneïs, qui fu avalez.
Par son le pont en est entrez, (3065-3068)
and
Lors s'en ist hors parmi la porte,
Mais ains qu'il par fust jus del pont,
Les piez de son cheval amont
Senti qu'il leverent en haut.
Et ses chevaux fist un grant salt. (3402-3406)

[23] Omer Jodogne ("L'Autre Monde Celtique dans la littérature française du XII° siècle" *Bulletin de la Classe des Lettres et des Sciences morales et politiques de l'Académie royale de Belgique*, 5th series, XLVI [1960], 584-597) starts with the assumption that Chrétien's Grail Castle is a representation of the Celtic Other World and then proceeds to modify his characterization of that realm based in part upon Chrétien's description of the Grail Castle.

Here then is the theory of Celtic origin — a hypothesis, which at first glance seems to be most comprehensive. But is this actually the case? Before examining the individual details of this thesis, a few remarks of a general nature are in order. I turn the discussion over to Professor Kenneth Jackson, a professional Celtologist. Professor Jackson cautions that, before advocating the Celtic thesis, it is indispensable to know the Celtic language and literature, to be able to read for oneself the texts in their original tongue. He notes that the authorities from whom the supporters of the Celtic theory confidently obtain information regarding Celtic literature, are often outdated by one or even two generations. Furthermore, even if the adherents of this theory should happen to chance upon a more recent source, it is quite possible that their lack of background will prevent them from correctly judging whether or not that source correctly represents Celtic thought and way of life. [24] In particular, nothing is more foreign to the Celtic way of life than the concept of courtly love. Furthermore, those who wish to see a basic pagan religious significance subjacent to the *Conte du Graal* err in their methodology, for the very myths considered by them to be "true guides to the most ancient pagan religious conceptions," and upon which these theorists have depended without reserve, are in reality nothing more than artificial reconstructions made by pseudo-historians at a time when Ireland had already been Christian for centuries. These "historians" have misunderstood the religious significance of the ancient legends from which they obtained their inspiration. [25]

Stefan Hofer further strengthens this warning by explaining that the basic problem of dating works of Celtic literature is a knotty one, with as much as five hundred years difference between estimates for the composition date of a given work. [26] He agrees with Professor Jackson that many of the sources used by the defenders of the Celtic thesis, are of a later date. [27] We should note in passing that these caveats do not, of course, preclude the possibility that "Celtic motifs," which perhaps were able to filter through various mythographical reworkings, may have influenced certain aspects of the Grail scene.

---

[24] Kenneth Jackson, "Les Sources celtiques du Roman du Graal," *Les Romans du Graal*, p. 214.
[25] Jackson, *Ibid.*, pp. 219-221.
[26] Hofer, *Chrétien de Troyes: Leben und Werke*, p. 36.
[27] Hofer, *Ibid.*, p. 208.

Let us now examine the Celtic hypothesis in a more precise manner. The first difficulty connected with this theory is that it lacks a unified textual source to serve as a frame of reference. [28] Though the Celtic theory does explain a large number of Chrétien's details, one must concede with Professor Vendryès that though the corpus of Irish literature (including the titles of lost texts) is quite well known, no single text has yet been found that could have served as a model for any of the continental Grail stories. [29] Stefan Hofer is in agreement on this point [30] as is Professor Jackson. These scholars claim that though there may be distant resemblances between individual Celtic motifs or talismans found in an amalgam of many different mythological sources, and certain objects found in *Le Conte du Graal*, there is no coherent Celtic tale which can be shown to have served either as the prototype or even as a vague outline for Chrétien's story. Indeed most supporters of the Celtic theory do not even claim that such a tale existed. "Rather than influences," Professor Vendryès believes, "we should speak of vague impressions. Celtic influence is minimal." [32]

Not only is the Celtic thesis, in effect, nothing more than a chain of individual motifs extracted from many different sources, but in addition great differences still exist between the individual Celtic talismans themselves and the objects of the Grail procession. Let us examine the properties of some of the magical articles of Celtic mythology to see if they resemble those of Chrétien's Grail scene. In my opinion, neither the cup in *The Phantom's Frenzy*, which contains ale, [33] nor the cup of the sea god Manannon in *The Adventures*

---

[28] Bruce, *The Origin of Arthurian Romance*, I, 275.
[29] M. Vendryès, "Remarques sur la communication de M. Jackson," *Les Romans du Graal*, p. 228; "Les Eléments celtiques de la légende du Graal," *Etudes Celtiques*, V (1949), pp. 1-50.
[30] *Chrétien de Troyes: Leben und Werke*, p. 209 n.
[31] "Les Sources celtiques," *Les Romans du Graal*, p. 226.
[32] Translations of his remarks, *Ibid.*, p. 228. However he does admit a "cas probable," Nuadu, whom he believes became the Fisher King. Stefan Hofer remarks, however, that no French *conteur* would even relate Celtic talismans with holy relics of the Grail legend nor associate any profound meaning with Celtic mythology (*Chrétien de Troyes: Leben und Werke*, p. 196).
[33] See Dillon, *Early Irish Literature*, p. 109; and Marx, *La Légende arthurienne et le Graal*, pp. 117-118, 275-276. The Irish text was edited by Pokorny in the *Zeitschrift für celtische Philologie*, XIII (1921), 371-382; and by Thurneysen, *Z.C.P.*, XX (1935), 213-227. A partial English translation may be found in Brown, *The Origin*, pp. 218-220.

of Cormac in the Land of Promise, which tests the veracity of a speaker,[34] nor the hamper of Gwyddneu Long Shank, which could supply the entire world with meat, provided groups of "thrice nine men should come around it at a time,"[35] bear sufficient resemblance to Chrétien's grail to warrant our classifying them as models. Neither could the Irish *criol* nor the drinking horn of Gwlgawd Gododdin have been the prototypes of the object described by Chrétien. The *criol*, unlike Chrétien's grail, was a magic coffer which contained jewels and clothing;[36] while the drinking horn had the properties of being inexhaustible and of being able to test truth in men and fidelity in women. The latter object was used for pouring drink on a wedding night,[37] and, again unlike Chrétien's grail, it was one of *many more than four* objects the search for which was imposed upon Kulhwch.[38] Marx explains that the drinking horn and the magic cup were often stolen in the middle of a banquet by a knight from the Other World. If Chrétien had in mind such talismans as his model, it would appear that he intended somehow to relate the cup which the Red Knight had stolen from Arthur at the beginning of the romance[39] to the grail.[40] This assumption is not textually justifiable.

The *dysgl* or platter of Rhydderch Hael, one of *thirteen* treasures of Britain, capable of dispensing to everyone whatever he desired in the way of food,[41] does not appear to have been Chrétien's model; and as for the cauldrons of plenty, they too, as we shall see, bear

---

[34] Dillon, *Early Irish Literature*, p. 112: "... if three lies are told over it, it breaks into three parts and three truths make it whole again." See also Loomis "The Irish Origin of the Grail Legend," *Speculum*, VIII (1933), 423; and Marx, *La Légende arthurienne et le Graal*, p. 118.

[35] Jones and Jones, The *Mabinogion*, p 115. This marvellous basket is reckoned amongst thirteen precious things of the Island of Britain in a manuscript of Mr. Justice Bosanquet where it is accredited with being able to feed 100 men if food for one man were put into it (Guest, *The Mabinogion*, p. 328).

[36] Brown, *The Origin*, pp. 440-448.

[37] Marx, *La Légende arthurienne et le Graal*, p. 124.

[38] Jones and Jones, *The Mabinogion*, p. 115.

[39] "Mais devant moi ma colpe prist
Et si folement l'en leva
Que sor la roïne versa
Tot le vin dont ele estoit plaine." (958-961)

[40] Marx, *La Légende arthurienne et le Graal*, pp. 124-125.

[41] Guest, *The Mabinogion*, p. 328; Marx, *La Légende arthurienne et le Graal*, p. 135.

little resemblance to the object in Chrétien's procession. In Irish and Welsh mythology, the latter would produce at will the most exquisite food, particularly pork and meat. They often contained fermented beer manufactured by the gods. One such object, the cauldron of the god Dagda, was one of four treasures which enabled the *Túatha Dé Danann* to defeat the Fomorians in *The Battle of Moytura* (*Cath Maige Tured*, in the mythological cycle).[42] Another cauldron — the one at the head of Annwfyn — did not boil the food of a coward.[43]

A third cauldron, possessed by Kyrridwen, was a generator of inspiration and knowledge,[44] while a cauldron mentioned in the tale *Branwen Daughter of Llyr* had the power of resurrecting the dead.[45]

Can these magic articles be our grail? Are they directly related to a bleeding lance? What relationship is there between the supernatural foods produced by these talismans — foods that can satisfy the entire world — and the sole host which is served to the ascetic on Chrétien's grail? Professor Frappier criticizes the defenders of the liturgical thesis because of the reverse order of the objects in the eucharistic procession in the Mass of St. John Chrysostom, a procession which contains a "lance," a "grail," and candles. But is there even a procession in the Celtic texts? Professor Frappier argues that Chrétien substituted a plate for a cauldron, a single host for a sumptuous banquet and justifies his opinion saying; "Il n'importe, une différence de forme

---

[42] Gustav Lehmacher, S. J., "Die zweite Schlacht von Mag Tured und die keltische Götterlehre," *Anthropos*, XXVI (1931), 435; Dillon, *Early Irish Literature*, pp. 58-62; and Marx, *La Légende arthurienne et le Graal*, pp. 136-137.

[43] This object is described in the poem "Preideu Annwfyn" in the *Book of Taliesin* (Jones and Jones, *The Mabinogion*, p. xxiii). The date of composition for this work is highly debatable with estimates ranging from the 8th century (Loomis) to the 12th and 13th centuries (F. Lot and Jones). See Hofer, *Chrétien de Troyes: Leben und Werke*, p. 36, and Jones and Jones (*The Mabinogion*, p. 115). Cf. the cauldron at Tyrnog, one of the thirteen treasures of Britian (Guest, *The Mabinogion*, p. 328).

[44] William Forbes Skene, ed. *The Four Ancient Books of Wales* (Edinburgh, 1862), II, 5-6, 145, 154-158; Marx, *La Légende arthurienne et le Graal*, p. 137.

[45] Jones and Jones, *The Mabinogion*, p. 29:
> 'I will enhance thy reparation still further' said Bendigeidfran. 'I will give thee a cauldron, and the virtue of the cauldron is this: a man of thine slain to-day, cast him into the cauldron, and by tomorrow he will be as well as he was at the best, save that he will not have the power of speech.'

Cf. Marx, *La Légende arthurienne et le Graal*, pp. 135-138, and p. 247.

ne saurait être un obstacle sérieux en la circonstance." [46] All that matters for him is the presence of a generative element in Chrétien's grail. But is that element really present?

> D'une sole oiste le sert on,
> Que l'en en cel graal le porte;
> Sa vie sostient et conforte,
> Tant sainte chose est le graals.
> Et il, qui est esperitax
> Qu'a se vie plus ne covient
> Fors l'oiste qui el graal vient. (6422-6428)

As we see from this passage, the grail does contribute a spiritual property to the host enabling it to sustain the ascetic's life, but it is also by the ascetic's own virtue that his life is sustained. Frappier, citing an example of Chrétien's use of the verb *venir* (referring to a fruit which *vient* on a tree — *Erec et Enide* v. 5400, ed. Foerster, v. 5352 ed. Roques) has advanced the claim that the grail generated the host. [47] However there are many questionable elements in this "proof." Professor Delbouille, commenting on Frappier's paper, remarks:

> ... si le texte d'*Erec,* parlant d'un fruit qui *vient* sur un arbre fournit un exemple de *venir* apparemment valable, le laconisme de Chrétien parlant de "l'oiste qui vient dans le graal" reste fort étrange! on ne s'attend pas à cela et un mot d'explication aurait bien été nécessaire pour le public le plus attentif et le plus subtil d'esprit. Pourquoi donc renoncer à comprendre comme on l'a toujours fait, quand le texte vient de dire quelques vers plus haut, que "l'on apporte l'hostie dans le graal" (v. 6423)? Si M. Frappier avait raison, à quoi rimeraient les allées et venues du *graal* à chaque service du repas? [48]

---

[46] *Perceval,* p. 94.
[47] "Le Graal et l'hostie," *Les Romans du Graal,* pp. 63-78, esp. p. 67. In both Roques's text (*Les Romans de Chrétien de Troyes, I: Erec et Enide,* Les Classiques français du Moyen Age, ed. Mario Roques [Paris, 1963], p. 163) and in Foerster's (*Erec und Enide von Christian von Troyes,* Vol. III, *Christian von Troyes sämtliche Werke nach allen bekannten Handschriften* [Halle, 1890], p. 193) there is no mention of a tree. The fruit grows (*vient*) on the fertile island of the castel of Brandigan. This observation, however, does not at all invalidate Frappier's argument.
[48] *Les Romans du Graal,* pp. 80-81.

A further difficulty inherent in this "proof," is that the example which Frappier cites is taken from the agricultural domain and that it is quite possible that Chrétien's use of *venir* in this sense was limited to the world of agriculture. Though Frappier counters this criticism by giving an instance where the old French verb *venir* is used in this sense outside the vegetable domain, it appears to me that his argument would have been more convincing had he been able to find this usage elsewhere in Chrétien's works, for as Professor Imbs reminds us, Old French is "une langue ... mouvante et susceptible de colorations individuelles." [49] As for the conjecture that the grail actually served the sumptuous foods to the Fisher King and to Perceval, even Professor Frappier is willing to concede that Chrétien's juxtaposition of the grail's passage and the serving of abundant foods does not *necessarily* imply a causal relationship between the two events (though later authors did interpret it as such). [50]

But let us pass on to an examination of the other articles in the Grail procession. The Celtic theorists have tried to explain the bleeding lance as a magic weapon which strikes, poisons and even predicts the future. [51] But can these talismans really be the lance of the Grail Castle, the "white lance" with a "white blade" from which "a drop of blood issued forth" (3197-3198)? Some have desired to see Chrétien's lance as one of the weapons of the god Lug [52] or the spear of King Pisear, which was kept in a cauldron that hissed and bubbled around it. [53] Marx identifies this flaming spear [54] with the *Gai Bolga* of Lug, who was master of thunder and lightning; with Oengus' bloody lance, and with the *Luin* of Celtchar whose force could only be attenuated by plunging it into a cauldron of poison and "black fluid." [55] But can

---

[49] "L'Elément religieux," *Les Romans du Graal*, p. 32.
[50] *Perceval*, pp. 95-96.
[51] See Marx, *La Légende arthurienne et le Graal*, pp. 129-135, 257-270.
[52] Lug's spear, "ihm oder jenem, der ihn trug, konnte niemand im Kampfe widerstehen," (Lehmacher, "Die zweite Schlacht," *Anthropos*, XXVI [1931], 439) or the stone with which Lug had pierced the only eye of the god Balor (King of the Fomorions) in *The Battle of Moytura* (Marx, *La Légende arthurienne et le Graal*, p. 130; cf. Dillon, *Early Irish Literature*, p. 60; and Lehmacher, p. 455) have oft been cited as models for Chrétien's lance, though the resemblance is far from satisfactory.
[53] Loomis, *The Grail: From Celtic Myth*, pp. 78-79.
[54] *Ibid.*, p. 79.
[55] *La Légende arthurienne et le Graal*, p. 131.

this protean object whose attributes are pieced together from a wide variety of texts, many of them (as for example the sixteenth-century *Fate of the Children of Turenn*)[56] posterior to Chrétien's work, be the *lance-qui-saigne?* Furthermore, the Irish "lance" was in actuality a javelin, i.e., it was normally thrown.[57] But, if this is the case, it is difficult to envisage it as the *lance* of the Grail procession since, as Professor Imbs demonstrates, Chrétien carefully distinguishes between a lance and a javelin: "Le Chevalier Vermeil frappe Perceval de sa lance (4129) et Perceval répond en le tuant d'un de ses javelots" (4151).[58] Professor Marx's implication that by the Celtic interpretation the javelin which had wounded the Fisher King may be equated with the *lance-qui-saigne*[59] appears to me completely arbitrary and unsubstantiated by Chrétien's text. But yet another difficulty threatens the defenders of the Celtic thesis. Though the Celtic theorists criticize those who believe the *lance-qui-saigne* is the Holy Lance on the grounds that the latter, unlike Chrétien's lance, which was destined to destroy the kingdom of Logres (6168-6171) did not possess a destructive quality,[60] these, same *celtisants,* with their purely maleficent lances, of which we have just seen several examples, would be hardpressed to account for the beneficent aspect of Chrétien's lance,[61]

---

[56] Dillon, *Early Irish Literature*, p. 62. He does note, however, that a summary of a cruder form of this story — perhaps dating back to the 11th century — exists. R. Thurneysen, the editor of that text ("Tuirell Bicrenn und seine Kinder," *Zeitschrift für celtische Philologie*, XII [1918], p. 243) estimates its date as being in the 12th century (though he admits the possibility of its having been composed a century earlier). Incidentally the weapon described there, though credited elsewhere with bleeding or shooting forth fire, does not resemble Chrétien's lance: "Der Speer Assals aus rotem gebuckeltem (?) Gold; der lebt nicht, dem er eine blutige Wunde schlägt, und man tut mit ihm keinen Fehlwurf, wenn man nur *ibar* ('Eibe') zu ihm sagt. Wenn man dann *altu-ibar* sagt, kommt er sofort zurück" (p. 247).
[57] Marx, *La Légende arthurienne et le Graal*, p. 130n.
[58] *Les Romans du Graal*, p. 49.
[59] *La Légende arthurienne et le Graal*, p. 130n.
[60] See Chapter One (esp. pp. 21, 22, and 31) for more details.
[61] For example:

"Come iés or mal aventurous
Quant tu tot che n'as demandé!
Que tant eüsses amendé
Le buen roi qui est mehaigniez
Que toz eüst regaaigniez
Ses membres et terre tenist,
Et si grans biens t'en avenist;" (3584-3590)

its association with Perceval's penitence [62] and its close relationship to the grail. [63]

Concerning the possible correspondence between the questions of the Sovranty of Ireland and those of Perceval, the Celtic theorists must admit with Frappier [64] that several difficulties preclude one's drawing a close parallel between the two texts. In the *Frenzy* there is no lance inside the house, though Lug is credited elsewhere with possessing one; there is no ascetic in the back room; the questions are asked, not by Conn, a visitor or non-initiate like Perceval, but by a beautiful, mystical lady. The food and drink served at the Phantom's banquet also differ from those of the Grail Castle repast. [65] "Mais des variantes de ce genre, qu'on rencontre dans tous les contes," remarks Frappier, "n'ont en général qu'une importance restreinte." [66] Perhaps, but the argument for the origin of Perceval's questions in *The Phantom's Frenzy* would be more convincing had the setting and the questions resembled those of *Le Conte du Graal* more closely.

The advocates of the Celtic theory had proposed the figure of the Sovranty of Ireland as the model for Chrétien's Grail Bearer. But they have difficulty in explaining the fact that most of the time this personage is depicted as an ugly witch and on one occasion as a girl whose initial ugliness changes to beauty [67] whereas Chrétien's Grail Bearer is a highly attractive girl. Despite the claims of Professors Brown [68] and Loomis, [69] there is no explicit statement on the part of Chrétien that the *Porteuse du graal* and the Loathly Damsel are the same person. Indeed in the Irish texts the esthetic transformation of the Sovranty of Ireland is from ugliness to beauty while in the *Conte du Graal*, if we assumed for argument's sake the identity of the Grail

---

and
"Que se tu demandé l'eüsses, [about the lance and the grail]
Li riches rois, qui or s'esmaie,
Fust ja toz garis de sa plaie
Et si tenist sa terre en pais." (4670-4673)

[62] "Por le pechié que tu en as
T'avient que rien n'en demandas
De la lance ne del graal" (6399-6401)
[63] See Chapter One (esp. p. 25).
[64] *Perceval*, p. 101.
[65] See Dillon, *Early Irish Literature*, p. 109.
[66] *Perceval*, p. 101.
[67] Brown, *The Origin of the Grail Legend*, pp. 210-224.
[68] Brown, *The Origin of the Grail Legend*, pp. 216-217.
[69] *The Grail: From Celtic Myth*, pp. 49-50.

Bearer with the Loathly Damsel, the transformation would be from beauty to ugliness.

According to Vendryès, Perceval's silence was the result of a *geis* as was his obligation to find a new lodging place every night.[70] But Professor Jackson cautions us against accepting such a proposition. He claims that the *geis* as a "magic spell cast upon the hero by another character in the story" occurs only in later romances such as *Diarmaid and Gráinne*,[71] or in modern popular stories. Its nature, however, was something entirely different in early Irish pagan stories. Due to the late appearance of the *geis* in Irish literature and due to its total absence in Welsh literature, Professor Jackson feels that it is highly improbable that the *geis* influenced Arthurian romance.[72]

We must also be prudent in quickly identifying the gods Bran or Nodens with the Fisher King. Admittedly there are resemblances, but there are also differences. As we have seen Bran's cauldron had the property of resurrecting dead warriors;[73] and Bran, unlike the Fisher King, was decapitated.[74]

Though the god Nuadu was wounded in *The Battle of Moytura*, it was an arm wound.[75] He possessed a sword which did not "bleed," and which was purely maleficent.[76] In *The Battle of Moytura* it is listed alongside a spear and a cauldron of abundance belonging to *someone else*.[77] But we have already concluded that Chrétien's grail does not resemble such a cauldron of plenty. Both Bran and Nodens were gods while the Fisher King, who was Perceval's cousin, was a flesh and blood human being. Professor Loomis, in order to find a Celtic model for the Fisher King, proposed a hypothetical prototype combining features of Bran with those of Lug:

---

[70] J. Vendryès, "Les Eléments celtiques de la légende du Graal," *Etudes Celtiques*, V (1949), 20.

[71] Dillon (*Early Irish Literature*, p. 42), explains that the earliest MS of this tale is from the seventeenth century though the story itself is mentioned in a tenth-century document.

[72] Jackson, "Les Sources celtiques," *Les Romans du Graal*, p. 219.

[73] J. Loth, *Les Mabinogion* (Paris, 1889), I, 75 and 89. Cf. note 45 of this chapter. Helaine Newstead claims that this personage was also credited with possessing an inexhaustible drinking horn from which he served guests (*Bran the Blessed*, pp. 11-20, 86-120, 125).

[74] Loth, *Les Mabinogion*, I, 90.

[75] Lehmacher, "De zweite Schlacht," p. 440.

[76] *Ibid.*, p. 439.

[77] *Ibid.*

> Can there be any reasonable doubt that Bran is the immediate prototype of the Fisher King; that he has taken over from Lug the role of the generous, supernatural host; and that his replacement has obscured the connection between *The Phantom's Frenzy* and the *Conte del Graal*? [78]

Unfortunately the diversity of his sources detracts from the effectiveness of his argument.

But as Professor Jackson observes, the entire approach of identifying an Arthurian character with one of the *Túatha Dé Danaan*, of assuming he was recognized as a god, of reconstructing his myth (from other sources) and then reinterpreting the events of the romance on the basis of this hypothetical myth is fallacious inasmuch as there is no proof that the *Túatha Dé Danaan* were ever recognized as gods of light and of goodness. Indeed the compilers of such tales such as *The Battle of Moytura* and *The Book of the Invasions* depicted these beings rather as prehistoric peoples. [79]

One final difficulty confronts the advocates of the theory of Celtic origin: How did the Irish tales reach Chrétien de Troyes? According to Professor Loomis their route would have been via Wales and Cornwall (which developed close relations with Ireland during the twelfth century), [80] through Armorica [81] and through Normandy. Professors Marx and Jackson prefer this latter route. [82]

But as Professor Hofer points out, these paths are highly questionable. Firstly, Arthur himself is unknown in Irish literature and only later does he appear in Welsh literature. Many Celtologists believe that the tale of Arthur's journey to Avalon and the related material first appeared with Geoffrey of Monmouth. Indeed one expert claims that the Arthurian references in *Kulhwch and Olwen* are "no necessary part of the romance." [83] Hofer reminds us that any hypothesizing of earlier Arthurian matter in Welsh literature should be viewed for

---

[78] *The Grail: From Celtic Myth to Christian Symbol*, p. 57.
[79] Jackson, "Les Sources celtiques," *Les Romans du Graal*, p. 221.
[80] "By What Route did the Romantic Tradition of Arthur Reach the French?" *Modern Philology*, XXXIII (1936), 225-238.
[81] *Arthurian Tradition and Chrétien de Troyes*, p. 471.
[82] See Jackson, "Les Sources celtiques," *Les Romans du Graal*, p. 225.
[83] W. J. Gruffydd, *The Mabinogion*. Transactions of the Hon. Soc. of Cymmrodorion (London, 1914), p. 32, cited by Hofer, p. 36.

THE THEORY OF CELTIC ORIGIN

what it is — conjecture. He states that we do not possess any Breton Arthurian texts prior to Geoffrey, neither do we have any evidence before Chrétien for the activity of Loomis' proposed *jongleur* "spreading... [Arthur's] fame." [84] Jackson, as we have seen, also remarks that we have no proof for the existence in Wales, Cornwall or Armorica of a coherent story resembling that of the Grail. [85]

Hofer feels that the social and political differences between the Norman conquerors and the British conquered precluded the exchange of any literary motifs between the two peoples. Though relations did begin to improve during the twelfth century, Hofer believes that it would have been inconceivable for a Celtic-French *Mischliteratur* to have existed. [86] He further asserts that the "evidence" for the existence of a widespread Arthurian tradition in England or on the Continent prior to Geoffrey, cannot withstand critical examination. For example, Herman of Tournai's testimony is of a later date. Likewise the debate over the date of the sculptures of the portal of the Modena cathedral has not been resolved. Indeed one authority believes the figures are from the middle of the twelfth century, while Hofer himself reminds us that it is also possible that the "Arthurian" names were added at a later date to already existing sculpted scenes. Similarly the Italian appellations "Artusius" and "Galvanus" may have been variations of other "non-Arthurian" names, etc., etc. [87]

As we have seen, the Christian and Celtic theorists not only present arguments that are extremely interesting in themselves but grapple with and attempt to resolve in a serious manner many of the enigmas presented by Chrétien's Grail procession. However, we have also observed that many difficulties arise if we attempt to interpret the Grail episode solely on the basis of any one of these theories. Should we then recognize, as do Professors Jackson, Nitze, and Loomis, the double nature — Christian and Celtic — of the Grail motif? [88] Perhaps,

---

[84] *Chrétien de Troyes: Leben und Werke*, pp. 35-36.
[85] "Les Sources celtiques," *Les Romans du Graal*, pp. 225-226.
[86] *Chrétien de Troyes: Leben und Werke*, pp. 36-37, 196. Jackson ("Les Sources celtiques," *Les Romans du Graal*, p. 226), however feels that it was possible in Normandy for such literary transmission to have taken place, though there is no proof that it occurred.
[87] See Hofer, pp. 36-39, for a full discussion of these "proofs." Cf. this chapter, note 2.
[88] Jackson, "Les Sources celtiques," *Les Romans du Graal*, p. 227. William A. Nitze, "Le Bruiden, le château du graal, et la lance-qui-saigne," *Ibid.*, pp. 291-292.

but, Professor Hofer would caution us against fusing these two elements. He believes, first of all, that the Passion relics are so far removed from the magical instruments of the Celts and that there was such a wide gap between the developed Christian literary tradition and the primitive Celtic one, that a fusion of the two would have been well-nigh impossible. [89] Furthermore, if one wanted to find *exact* parallels between elements of these two traditions and the objects of Chrétien's Grail scene, one would be forced to extract individual motifs from such a large number of texts that the credibility of the argument would greatly suffer. The following citation from Loomis graphically illustrates this point:

> *Le Conte del Graal* is a highly complex pattern, to which the *enfances* of Cuchulainn, the story of Finn's birth, his vengeance and his meeting with his uncle, the account of Conn's visit to the palace of Lug and the Sovranty of Erin, Welsh traditions of the wounded King Bran and his brother Beli, of a castle of Ladies on the Severn, and of meetings and combats with the proud huntsman Arawn have all contributed. Besides these Celtic contributions of primary importance there are, as we have observed, minor features and incidents which are paralleled in the extant Irish and Welsh literature of the Middle Ages. In spite of the great gaps in our knowledge about Bran, Beli. Pryderi, Gwri, Llwch, Modron and Riannon, it is surprising how much can be pieced together from the scraps of information we possess, and how neatly those patterns conform, despite rationalization and confusion, to those present in Chrétien's work.... These tales, gradually adapted to French tastes, given a new localization in Anglo-Norman Britain after the Conquest were the great sensations of the twelfth century.... Linked into more or less coherent long narratives and written down in prose, they furnished Chrétien with his *matière*. [90]

Perhaps, as Professor Vendryès indicates, the themes of *Le Conte du Graal* are none other than universal folk motifs which cannot be precisely situated in time or space. [91] Such an explanation would appear to be the most valid. But before hastily passing final judgment,

---

[89] *Chrétien de Troyes: Leben und Werke*, p. 208.
[90] Roger Sherman Loomis, *Arthurian Tradition and Chrétien de Troyes* (New York, 1949), pp. 467-468.
[91] *Les Romans du Graal*, p. 228.

let us examine a new theory which I intend to propose in the next chapter. In my opinion this theory will have the dual advantage of explaining a greater number of details in Chrétien's Grail scene (the questions, the dual nature of the bleeding lance, the grail, its female bearer, etc.) while at the same time being based upon a unified and clearly delineated corpus.

CHAPTER III

A NEW JUDAIC INTERPRETATION

For over three thousand years, the Jewish people annually commemorated the Exodus from Egypt by means of the Passover festival, the "Feast of Redemption." During the Mishnaic Period (ca. 100 B.C. to 200 A.D.) the institutional observance of this event was fixed in the form of a family banquet which is today called the *Seder* by Ashkenazic (German and East European) Jews and *Haggadah* by their Sephardic (Spanish or Portuguese) coreligionists. Certain ritual acts were prescribed for the observance of this ceremony. In the first part of this chapter I should like to suggest that Chrétien de Troyes may have had in mind just such a banquet (especially in its Sephardic form) when he composed his description of the repast at the Fisher King's castle. In the second portion of this chapter I shall attempt to demonstrate that it was possible for Chrétien to have had either direct or indirect knowledge of the *Seder* ritual.

In describing the various customs associated with the *Seder*, I shall refer to medieval Hebraic texts. These sources together with biblical, talmudic, and midrashic passages as well as citations from the Passover evening ritual prayer book (also called the *Haggadah*)[1] should be regarded as highly important, since these were known during Chrétien de Troyes's time. I shall also make reference to sociological studies of the practices of certain modern and contemporary Sephardic Jewish communities, as well as to the transcription of personal interviews that I conducted with members of the Aleppo Syrian Jewish community of Brooklyn, New York, during the spring of 1968. These sources too are of great value since the strong group cohesiveness of

---

[1] In this study I shall use the term *Seder* to refer to the banquet, and *Haggadah* to refer to the prayer book.

PLATE 7. Passover Plate. Pewter. Master G. R. van Go., 1718.

PLATE 3. Passover Plate. Pewter. Alsace-Lorraine, 18th Century.

the *Sephardim* throughout the centuries precluded major changes in their religious practices.[2] Wherever possible, I shall employ such sociological evidence in conjunction with related textual sources.

PART ONE

THE "SEDER" AS A MODEL FOR CHRÉTIEN'S GRAIL EPISODE

Before examining Chrétien's text, let us take a quick glance at the *Seder* ritual. The Bible proclaims, "And on that day you will explain to your son, 'This is because of what Yahweh did for me when I came out of Egypt'" (Exodus 13:8). The *Seder* was established to fulfill this didactic imperative. This banquet is held on the first two nights of the eight-day Passover festival.[3] According to the liturgical order for the evening (the word *Seder* itself means "order" in Hebrew), a series of questions traditionally asked by the youngest present, occasions the recounting of the Exodus story (both in its biblical and talmudic forms) by the head of the household. The ceremonial meal proper (patterned after the ancient Greco-Roman banquets of mishnaic times) follows, and concluding psalms and poems are then recited.

Though many of the evening's practices (e.g., the eating of unleavened bread, the drinking of wine, the reclining position assumed by the participants, etc.) are explicitly ordained in either biblical or rabbinic sources, minor variants do exist — either in the text of the *Haggadah* itself[4] and in the directions associated with it[5] or in

---

[2] See, for example: Abraham A. Neuman, "Sephardim," *The Universal Jewish Encyclopedia* (New York, 1943), IX, 477-478; Meyer Kayserling, "Sephardim," *The Jewish Encyclopedia* (New York, 1901), XI, 197-198. Cf. Walter P. Zenner ("Syrian Jews in Three Social Settings," *The Jewish Journal of Sociology*, X [1968], 117): "In New York the occupational specialization and interdependence of Syrian Jews makes the Syrian group relatively cohesive...." Subsequent research which I conducted in Israel on Jews who originated in Aleppo (*Ḥaleb*), Syria confirm the existence of the same practices as those of their Brookyn coreligionists which I shall describe in this chapter.

[3] In the Holy Land where the festival lasts for seven days, only one *Seder* is held, on the first night.

[4] E. D. Goldschmidt classifies them into 6 different groups (*The Passover Haggadah: Its Sources and History* [in Hebrew], [Jerusalem, 1960], p. 3).

[5] See Menaḥem M. Kasher and Shemuel Ashkenazi, eds., *Haggadah Sheleimah* (Jerusalem, 1961), pp. 17-222, for a full discussion of the rabbinic sources pertaining to the order of the evening.

the exact manner of executing certain prescribed gestures. We shall discuss these more fully during our re-examination of Chrétien's Grail episode. Let us now return to this fascinating text.

When Perceval enters the main hall of the Grail Castle he finds the Fisher King seated on a bed, reclining upon his elbow:

> Ens enmi la sale en un lit
> Un bel preudome seoir vit,
> ... ...
> Apoiez fu desor son coute. (3085-3086, 3092)

Though the nobleman may have been in this position because of his infirmity, Chrétien does not explicitly say so. It is most interesting, however, to observe that traditional Jewish law specifically ordains that during the *Seder* one is to recline upon one's elbow as a symbol of freedom:

> Le soir du Sédère tous les israélites sont allongés, même le plus pauvre en Israel ne doit manger autrement qu'accoudé (Pessa'him X, 1): Tous doivent se sentir des hommes libres en célébrant la délivrance de nos ancêtres de l'esclavage d'Egypte. [6]

Since this custom is mentioned in the Mishnah (*Pesaḥim* X, 1), we do not have to go further to demonstrate that it was known during the time of Chrétien de Troyes. However, to assure ourselves of its practice at that period let us read from *Sepher Pardes Hagadol*, a compilation of laws, customs, and responsa generally attributed to the great biblical and talmudic commentator Rashi, Rabbi Shelomoh ben Yitzḥak of Troyes (1040-1105): [7]

ונסדר מפי רבינו שלמה ז"ל ... ושותין בהסיבת שמאל דרך חירות ...
ואוכלין בהסיבה.[8]

---

[6] Robert Nerson, *La Haggada commentée: traduction et commentaire du texte intégral de la Haggada de Pâque; explication des usages du sédère* (Paris, 1966), p. 5.

[7] Henri Gross (*Gallia Judaica* [Paris, 1897], p. 228), believes that many of the decisions of *Sepher Pardes Hagadol* were composed by Shemayah, the disciple of Rashi, though portions of another work of Rashi (*Sepher Haorah*) are found in it. He also notes that the book contains subsequent additions, as, for example, decisions of Yoseph ibn Plat, who lived in Lunel at the end of the twelfth century.

[8] *Sepher Pardes Hagadol Vesepher Haorah*, eds. Mikhael Levi Frumkin and Yitzḥak Finkelstein (Warsaw, 1870; [Jerusalem]: Mephitzei Or, [1959]), p. 52, paragraph 132.

And it was ordained by Rabbi Shelomoh of Blessed Memory.... One drinks reclining to the left side as a free man and one eats reclining.

Similarly, the late 12th-century rabbi, Avraham ben Rabbi Natan Hayarḥi ("of Lunel") in *Sepher Hamanhig,* a collection of Jewish religious customs practiced in European countries (written in Toledo, 1204-1205),[9] remarks:

עו) ... ושותין בהסיבה דרך חירות.
עז) ... ויאכל בהסיבה דרך חירות.[10]

76) ... One drinks [wine] reclining as a free man
77) ... One eats [unleavened bread] reclining as a free man.

Sephardic Jews in the Middle Ages practised this same custom as the following citation from *Sepher Abudarham* demonstrates:

ושותה כל אחד מהם כוסו בהסבה דרך חירות.[11]

Everyone drinks his cup reclining as a free man.

This work was composed by Rabbi David ben Rabbi Yoseph of Seville, in 1359. It is still used today by Sephardic Jews.

Illustrations of figures in a reclining position can be found in many medieval illuminated *Haggadah* manuscripts.[12]

---

[9] See Gross, *op. cit.,* p. 283, for a biography of the author.

[10] *Sepher Hamanhig* (Jerusalem, 1967), p. 134, paragraphs 76 and 77.

[11] *Sepher Abudarham* (Rabbi M. A. Kempler, USA), p. 117 (fol. 59).

[12] For example the late thirteenth or early fourteenth-century Sephardic *Haggadah* (British Museum Or. 2737) contains an illumination (folio 91) in which "les deux figures de droite et de gauche s'appuient visiblement sur de petits coussins clairs" (Mendel Metzger, "La Haggada enluminée," thesis, University of Poitiers, 1961. Bibliothèque Universitaire de Poitiers 350-728 5-1961; Bibliothèque du Centre d'Etudes Supérieures de Civilisation Médiévale, Université de Poitiers; l. 1961. 1 [vols. 1 and 2 only], I, 101. N. B. In the summer of 1968, when I was able to continue my research in France, only the copy in the CESCM library was available. Cf. Mendel Metzger, *La Haggada enluminée,* Vol. I, *Etude iconographique et stylistique des manuscrits enluminés et décorés de la Haggada du XIIIe au XVIe siècle.* Etudes sur le judaïsme médiéval, No. 2 [Leiden, 1973], p. 82 and Plate XII, fig. 54). See also the illustration of the "Sages of Benei Brak and the Family *Seder* Scene in the 14th century" illuminated Haggadah British Museum Add 14761 described by Rachel Wischnitzer ("Passover in Art," *The Passover Anthology,* ed. Philip Goodman [Philadelphia, 1961], pp. 297-298 and 301) or the family *Seder* scenes in the 14th century, Sarajevo *Haggadah* (*Ibid.,* p. 300). Cf. Plate 2 in our study.

It was furthermore customary at the *Seder* to recline on a bed or divan as a sign of liberty. Attestation of this custom may be found in another citation from Hayarḥi:

בבוא איש מבית מקדש מעט ומצא...
מטות מוצעות ונרות דולקות (sic).[13]

On one's return from the synagogue one [should] find ... the beds spread out and candles lit.

In Chrétien's narrative Perceval joins the Fisher King upon the bed, which was near a fire:

> S'ot devant lui un fu molt grant
> ... ...
> Li vallés s'est lez lui assis,
> ... ...
> Et cels qui el lit se seoient; (3093, 3119, 3195)

and in Manessier's continuation Perceval also holds his head in an inclined position:

> Pierchevaus, ki ot désiervi
> C'on fesist de lui joie et feste
> Tenoit embroncie la teste.[14]

Though one cannot, of course, clarify details in Chrétien's narrative on the basis of Grail stories later than Chrétien's, what Frappier has to say on the matter is worthy of note:

> Il [Chrétien] déclare lui-même qu'il utilisait un livre donné par Philippe d'Alsace. Dans ces conditions, il n'est pas interdit de croire que les continuateurs ont renoué avec la source de Chrétien ou avec des contes analogiques....[15]

---

[13] *Sepher Hamanhig*, p. 129, paragraph 56.

[14] Charles Potvin, ed., *Perceval le Gallois ou le Conte du Graal, publié d'après les manuscrits originaux, Deuxième Partie: Le Poème de Chrétien et de ses continuateurs d'après le manuscrit de Mons.* Société des Bibliophiles Belges séant à Mons, Publication No. 21 (Mons, 1871), V, vv. 34948-34950.

[15] *Perceval*, pp. 96-97. Frappier's statement is of course dependent upon the veracity of Chrétien's admission that he was elaborating upon an already existing story (66-67; Cf. Introduction, note 2). The Manessier continuation in particular offers many interesting readings which I shall discuss later.

As Perceval is seated next to the Fisher King in Chrétien's account, four different objects are paraded before the eyes of the young knight. Because he fails to ask questions, tragic results are destined to befall his host and his host's people. For Chrétien the number four may have had significance in relation to the Grail banquet, since he employs it many times in his description of this scene.[16] It is interesting, however to note that in the symbolism of the *Seder* the number four plays an important role. *Four* questions must be asked by the youngest present, and *four* cups of wine must be imbibed during the course of the banquet. These correspond according to Rabbi Benaya (*Yer. Pesaḥim* 376) to the *four* expressions of Redemption found in Exodus 6:6-7.[17] In the evening's liturgy there are allegorical descriptions of *four* types of sons, and during the *Seder* one is required to partake of *four* types of food.[18] Now, if we examine each of the objects in Chrétien's procession we find that they too have their place in the *Seder*.

The Questions and the Grail

In our first chapter we saw the extreme importance of the questions in *Le Conte du Graal*; and we noted that neither of the two theories of Christian origin could account for them, while in our second chapter we observed that the questions in *The Phantom's Frenzy* proposed by the adherents of the theory of Celtic origin to have been Chrétien's model, were not at all analogous to those that Perceval was supposed to ask.

In the Passover *Seder,* however, questions very similar to Perceval's play a most important role. At the beginning of the evening certain unusual actions must be performed so as to elicit questions by the youngest present. These questions are extremely important, since, in answering them, the head of the household fulfills the requirement of

---

[16] Four servants greet Perceval (3070), four columns support the hood of the fireplace (v. 3095), four hundred men could sit near the fire (3096), and four servants remove the Fisher King at the conclusion of the meal (vv. 3344-3345).

[17] I will free you ... I will release you ... I shall deliver you ... I will adopt you.... See also *La Haggada commentée,* p. 3; and *Haggadah Sheleimah,* p. 90.

[18] Pesaḥ, matzah, maror, and ḥaroset.

recounting the story of the Exodus from Egypt.[19] Though the form of these questions was fixed at the end of the Mishnaic period, spontaneous questions were, and still are, encouraged. The latter could at times even exempt one from posing the traditional formal questions. At the time of Chrétien de Troyes, the formal questions were required to be repeated in French so that they would be comprehensible to all present.[20]

In the Aleppo Syrian Jewish community of Brooklyn, New York, the following custom may be observed.[21] A young girl of marriageable age (usually a daughter of the officiant, if he is head of the household) takes the *Seder* plate away from the table and carries it in her hands to another room (e.g., the kitchen). The youngest present after asking the four traditional questions, calls out "Where are you going? Why did you remove the plate; we have not yet begun to eat dinner?" The young lady then returns the plate to the table and the master of the house (the officiant) begins to recount the story of the Exodus.

Other modern Sephardic *Seder* services similarly require that the *Seder* plate be taken away from the table to arouse the curiosity of the youngest present. Frija Zuarts, in a study of the religious practices of Libyan Jews reports that at their *Seder* a *woman* takes the plate from the table and carries it above the heads of all those present so as to "elicit questions" from the youngest present.[22] A Spanish *Haggadah* specifies (in Judeo-Spanish [Ladino]):

אי קיטאראן איל פלאטו די לה מיזה אי דיראן מה נשתנה... מסבין
אי טורנאראן איל פלאטו אין לה מיזה אי דיראן עבדים היינו....[23]

---

[19] Professor Urban T. Holmes makes a fleeting allusion to these questions but quickly abandons them saying, "We are not forcing a comparison between the Passover and the Grail" (*A New Interpretation of Chrétien's Conte del Graal,* University of North Carolina Studies in the Romance Languages and Literatures, No. 8 [Chapel Hill, 1948], p. 21).

[20] *Sepher Pardes Hagadol,* p. 53, paragraph 133:

> And one says the "Haggadah," that is, *Ha Laḥma Anya* ("This is the bread of affliction") and *Mah Nishtanah* ("Why is this night different?" — the opening line of the four questions), in the language of the country in which one resides.

[21] See Plate 3 for a reproduction of the *Ha Laḥma Anya* passage from a fourteenth-century MS. The description of this ritual is based on accounts given me by three members of this community: Messrs. S. Tawil, S. Sutton and F. Beda.

[22] Frija Zuartz (פריג'א זוארץ), "Miminhagei Yahadut Luv," *Yalkut Minhagim,* ed. Avraham Ben-Yaakov (Jerusalem, 1967), p. 87:

And they shall take away the plate from the table and say "Why is this night different...."

And they shall return the plate to the table and say "We were slaves" (the opening words of the ritual Exodus Story):

while a more recent Tunisian *Haggadah* instructs:

> On emporte le plateau.
> ... ...
> On rapporte le plateau.²⁴

בשו"ע או"ח סימן תמ"ג בסעיף ו' כתוב שיסלקו את הקערה מעל השולחן כדי שיראו התינוקות וישאלו. והנה נוסף להגבהת הקערה נוהגים שבעלת הבית מסובבת אותה על ראשי כל בני המשפחה ואפילו על ראשו של התינוק הישן בעריסתו. סיבוב זה נעשה תוך קריאת הפסקה "מה נשתנה".

In the First Treatise of the Code of Jewish Laws (*Shulḥan Arukh: Oraḥ Ḥayyim*) chapter 443, paragraph 6 it is written: that the *Seder* plate be removed from upon the table so that the children will see it and ask [questions]. Here, in addition to lifting up the *Seder* plate, it is the custom that the mistress of the house rotate it above the heads of all members of the household, even above the head of a baby sleeping in its cradle. This rotation is done during the reading of the four questions.

²³ *Haggadah shel Pesaḥ kephi Minhag Hasepharadim*

הגדה של פסח כפי מנהג הספרדים וצ"ו איסטאמפאדה קון ליטרא אירמוצה אי לאדינאדה מוי ביין אי קאמפלידה אין סדר אינטירו די לה מגי ועם ציורים נאים ויפים הנחמדים למראה עין צופים.

(Vienna: Joseph Schlesinger, n.d.), p. 19.

I propose the following transcription for the above citation:

y quitarán el plato de la mesa y dirán:

מה נשתנה... מסביןּ

y tornarán el plato en la mesa y dirán:

עבדים היינו.

²⁴ David Berdah, tr., *La Haggada de Pâque avec traduction et commentaires en langue française* (Tunis, 1957), p. 19. N.B. Cecil Roth (*Haggada for Passover Copied and Illustrated by Ben Shaan with a Translation, Introduction and Historical Notes by Cecil Roth* [New York and Paris, 1965], p. 14), Mordecai Lubelsky ("At a Seder in Casablanca," *The Day Jewish Journal*, The Sunday Review [April 20, 1958], Section III, p. 4), and J. D. Eisenstein, (*Otzar Peirushim Vetziyurim el Haggadah Shel Pesaḥ* [New York, 1920], pp. 337-338) describe a Moroccan custom of having a member of the household carry the *Seder* plate past every participant waving it over each person's head. The latter author notes (p. 338) that in the Yemenite *Seder* at the time of the recounting of the Exodus, the small table which is before the participants is removed.

Similarly Avraham Ben-Yaakov recounts that among the Babylonian Jews the head of the household commands that the *Seder* plate be removed so that the son may ask in Hebrew, "Why do you command that the *Seder* plate be removed before we have eaten? Why is this night different from all other nights?"[25] This custom rests upon a strong textual basis, Hayarḥi explains:

ובעת שמתחילין ההגדה (sic)   עוקרין את השלחן כדי שישאלו הנערים
בדכתבו בע״פ מניחין שלחן ומצה לפני כל אחד ואחד ומרור לפני כל אחד
ואחד ואין עוקרים את השלחן אלא לפני מי שאומר ההגדה. ואמרו אביי חזא דקא
מדלי תכא פי דקא מגבהי פתורא אמר אכתי לא אכלינן דעקריתי תקא מקמן
א״ל רבה פטרתן מלומר מה נשתנה וה״מ לדידהו שהיו להם שלחנות קטנות
(sic)   אבל אנו שהשלחנות שלנו גדולים ואין דבר קל לסלקן אנו מסלקין
הכל (sic)   עם המצות ומרורין והתבשילין ודי לנו בכך.[26]

At the time when one begins the *Haggadah* ('recounting of the Exodus') the table is taken away so that the youngsters will ask questions as it is written in the chapter "The Eves of Passover" (*Pesaḥim* X), a table and unleavened bread are placed before everyone, and bitter herbs before everyone and only the table before the one who recites the *Haggadah* is taken away. And it was recounted that Abaya [as a child] seeing that the parsley was removed asked straightaway "Why is the parsley taken away, we have not yet begun to eat?" Rabah said he is thus exempted from asking the formal questions. But this custom was applicable in their time when they had small tables. But in our time when the tables are large and it is not easy to remove them, we remove the basket with the unleavened bread and bitter herbs and food. And this is sufficient for us.

Similarly Abudarham prescribes:

וכשאומר הא לחמא עניא עוקרין הסל או הקערה מעל השלחן כדי שיכירו
התינוקות וישאלו מה נשתנה הלילה הזה מכל הלילות שבכל הלילות אנו אכלין
מה שלפנינו בקערה ועכשיו היא מסולקת מלפנינו... ובהשלמת הא לחמא
עניא יחזיר הסל או הקערה למקומה כדי שתהיה לפניו כשאמר ההגדה.[27]

---

[25] Avraham Ben-Yaakov, "Miminhagei Yahadut Bavel," *Yalkut Minhagim*, p. 33:

לאחר אמירת "הא לחמא עניא" שלושה פעמים... מצווה האב להרחיק את הקערה וכאן הבן שואל: מדוע אתה מצווה להסיר את הקערה לפני שאכלנו? "מה נשתנה"

After the recitation of [the passage] "This is the bread of affliction" three times, the father commands that the *Seder* plate be taken away, whereupon the son asks "Why do you command that the *Seder* plate be removed before we have eaten? Why is this night different from all other nights?"

[26] *Sepher Hamanhig*, p. 133, paragraph 70.

[27] *Sepher Abudarham*, p. 118. Cf. J. D. Eisenstein, ed., *Otzar Peirushim Vetziyurim el Haggadah shel Pesaḥ*. A compendium (in Hebrew) of author-

When [the paragraph of] "This is the bread of affliction" is said, the basket or plate is taken away from the table so that the children will notice [it] and ask "Why is this night different from all [other] nights, for on all [other] nights we eat what is before us on the plate and now it is removed from before us?" At the conclusion of [the paragraph of] "This is the bread of affliction," the basket or plate is returned to its place.

If we interpret Chrétien's procession in terms of this custom, the grail would be the *Seder* plate (*kearah* in Hebrew), its female bearer would be the "young girl of marriageable age" (the daughter of the master of the house), and the questions would be those the youngest present is supposed to ask at the time of the removal of the *kearah*.

Evidence seems to indicate that a *grail* was commonly understood to be a type of plate. Mario Roques notes that the first mention of such a receptacle is found in the Venice manuscript of the *Roman d'Alexandre* where a pilgrim says to his host "Ersoir mangai o toi a ton graal." [28]

Mario Roques explained that in this context such a word could signify either an *écuelle* from which it was customary for two people to eat together or a *plat* into which several guests could place their hands simultaneously (as did Jesus at the last supper and as Orientals still do at ceremonial meals). He preferred the latter interpretation. [29] Hélinand de Froidmont's thirteenth-century definition, cited in Chapter One, describes a grail as a wide dish with a little depth to it (*"scutella lata aliquantulum profunda"*), upon which festive foods were served. [30] The Grail Cycle of Robert de Boron, the *Lancelot-Graal (L'Estoire*

---

itative commentaries and original illustrations on the Haggada (New York, 1920), pp. 169-170.

[28] *Le Roman d'Alexandre*, ed. Milan S. LaDu (Princeton, 1937), v. 618. The earlier *Alexandre décasyllabique* (see *The Medieval French Roman d'Alexandre*, III, *Version of Alexandre de Paris* [Princeton, 1941], ed. Alfred Foulet, Elliott Monographs, XXXVIII, 1-100) which is recognized to be the source of the archetype of the A (Arsenal), B (Venice), and L (Paris) MSS gives the following reading for v. 611:

Ot tei manchai erser a ton graal (p. 91).

[29] Mario Roques, *Le Graal de Chrétien et la Demoiselle au Graal*, Publications Romanes et Françaises, No. 50 (Geneva, 1955), pp. 1-2.

[30] P.L. CCXII, cols. 814-815. Cf. Chapter One, p. 22.

del *Saint Graal, L'Estoire de Merlin, La Queste*), and in part the *Perlesvaus* specifically identify this object with the plate of the Last Supper (also a *kearah*) and compare the Grail Table with the table of Jesus' final meal.[31] The nature of the *Seder* plate on the other hand could very well correspond to Hélinand's definition of a grail since Abudarham equates the term *kearah* with *sal* "basket"[32] while Hayarḥi employs exclusively the latter term in referring to the *Seder* plate. On the *Seder* plate are pieces of unleavened bread which *may* correspond to the Mass wafer carried upon the grail.

Though I have not as yet been able to find a rabbinic text which specifies that a *girl must* remove the *Seder* plate (N.B. neither does Chrétien specify that only a *girl must* carry the grail), one may assume however that women would most often perform such a function, related to the serving of the meal. This is the case in a fourteenth-century *Haggadah* (British Museum Add. 14761) where an illumination illustrating the passage "This is the bread of affliction" (which immediately precedes the questions) depicts a servant girl carrying the

---

[31] In *L'Estoire de Merlin*, for example, Merlin asks Uther Pendragon to construct a third table "à l'image des saintes tables de la Cène et du Graal. Ce sera la Table Ronde" (Marx, *La Légende arthurienne et le Graal*, p. 352) while in *L'Estoire del Saint Graal* the "Table du Saint Graal" is "renouveleé de la table de la Cène" (*Ibid.*, p. 35). Marx (*Nouvelles Recherches sur la littérature arthurienne* [Paris, 1965], pp. 9, 16, 19, 39-43, 64-67, 139-166) discusses the matter fully. He sees the grail as a fusion of Celtic and "Christian" traditions.

[32] See the last citation from Abudarham above on pp. 58-59. Cf.

מביאין לפניו סל או קערה...

"A basket or plate is brought before him (*Sepher Abudarham*, p. 116)." Metzger ("La Haggada enluminée," thesis, I, 142, n. 19; Cf. *La Haggada enluminée*, I: *Etude iconographique*... [Leiden, 1973], pp. 110, n. 2; 112, n. 1) notes that in Sephardic *Haggadot* the word *sal* is used instead of *Kearah*). N.B. The interlinear gloss of the Rouen MS of the 11th century grammarian Yonah ibn Janaḥ's hebraic root dictionary (*Kitab al Uṣul*), defines *kearah* as زبديّة (bowl) and قصعة (large bowl) —Adolf Neubauer, ed., *The Book of Hebrew Roots by Abu'l Walîd Marwân ibn Janâh, called Rabbi Jonâh*, (Amsterdam, 1968), col. 640. The Latin marginal gloss in the Naples edition of David Kimḥi's 12th century root dictionary renders *kearah* as *scutella* (*Thesaurus Linguae Sanctae ex R. David Kimchi. Sepher Hashorashim*, ed. Sanctus Pagninus [Naples, 1548], p. 1173). Professor Holmes has suggested a resemblance between Hélinand's *gradalus* and the *Seder* plate (*Chrétien de Troyes*, p. 166). See Plates 3, 5, 6, 7, 8, 9, 10 for reproductions of *Seder* plates.

cloth-covered *Seder* basket.³³ Though Chrétien does not specify the Grail Maiden's identity, the Manessier continuation explains that she is the daughter of the Fisher King and that she is a virgin. What is still more interesting however, is that according to the Montpellier MS the female Grail Bearer is Jewish (a descendant of Israel):

> Cele ki porta le Gréal,
> Si est du lignage Israel
> Pucile virgene;....³⁴

which may indicate that the Fisher King is also of the Jewish persuasion.

Finally, Perceval's unasked questions resemble much more closely the questions asked by the youngest [male] present (a non-initiate like Perceval) than those of the Sovranty of Ireland. It is also most noteworthy that in the liturgy of the *Haggadah*, shortly after the questions are asked, there is a parable, which speaks of a *son who does not know how to ask (Haben Sheeino Yodea Lishol);* — cf. Plate 1 —

---

³³ Rachel Wischnitzer, "Passover in Art," *The Passover Anthology*, Philip Goodman, ed. (Philadelphia, 1961), p. 301. N.B. Since Chrétien does not describe the contents of the grail when Perceval first sees it and only later specifies that the grail was *trestot descovert* ("unveiled"), it appears reasonable to assume that the grail, just as the *Seder* plate, was covered at the time of its first appearance.

Alexandre Micha ("Le Graal et la Lance," *Romania*, LXXIII [1952], 464) likewise offers the interpretation that the grail (which according to him is a *pyxide* in the communion of a moribund person) was covered the first time Perceval saw it. He thus disagrees with Frappier who interprets the expression *trestot descovert* (describing the grail) as meaning "very apparent" ("Sur l'interpretation du vers 3301 du *Conte du Graal*," *Romania*, LXXI [1950], 240-245; "Autres remarques sur le vers 3301 du *Conte du Graal*," *Bulletin bibliographique de la Société Internationale Arthurienne*, II [1950], 89-93, "Encore le 'Graal trestot descovert,'" *Romania*, LXXII [1951], 236-238; Du 'Graal trestot descovert' à la forme du Graal chez Chrétien de Troyes," *Romania*, LXXIII [1952], 82-92). Note, however, that Frappier vigorously defends himself in *Romania*, LXXXIV (1953), 358-375 ("Du 'Graal trestot descovert' à l'origine de la légende"). Cf. Chapter Two, note 24. It is furthermore interesting to observe that the above-cited *Haggadah* MS contains a series of illustrations commencing with an illumination depicting a procession of men displaying the symbolic foods (Goodman, *The Passover Anthology*, Fig. 7; and Plate 13 in our study).

³⁴ Charles Potvin, ed., *Perceval le Gallois ou le Conte du Graal publié d'après les manuscrits originaux*; Deuxième Partie: *Le Poème de Chrétien de Troyes et de ses continuateurs d'après le manuscrit de Mons*, Société des Bibliophiles Belges séant à Mons, Publication No. 21 (Mons, 1870), V, vv. 35161-35163.

exactly the case of Perceval. We shall have more to say about this parable in the fifth chapter.

The Bleeding Lance

In Chrétien's procession a *lance-qui-saigne* preceded the grail:

> Uns vallés d'un[e] chambre vint,
> Qui une blanche lance tint
> Empoignie par le milieu,
> Si passa par entre le feu
> Et cels qui el lit se seoient.
> Et tot cil de laiens veoient
> Le lance blanche et le fer blanc,
> S'issoit une goute de sanc
> Del fer de la lance en somet,
> Et jusqu'a la main au vallet
> Coloit cele goute vermeille. (3191-3201)

The proponents of the Christian theses, as we saw, were unable to account for its bleeding, while both the Celtic and Christian theorists (for opposite reasons) were unable to explain its simultaneously beneficent and maleficent nature. However, if we view this object from the perspective of the *Seder*, we find that both these difficulties are obviated. To begin with, blood played an important role in the biblical Passover:

> Some of the blood [of the Paschal sacrifice] must then be taken and put on the two doorposts and the lintel of the houses.... When I see the blood I will pass over you and you shall escape the destroying plague when I strike the land of Egypt.
> ... ...
> Dip it [a spray of hyssop] in the blood that is in the basin and with the blood from the basin touch the lintel and the two doorposts.... Then when Yahweh goes through Egypt to strike it and sees the blood on the lintel and on the two doorposts, he will pass over the door and not allow the destroyer to enter your homes and strike. You must keep these rules as an ordinance for all time for you and your children. (Exodus 12:7 and 12; 21-25) [35]

---

[35] J. B. Segal (*The Hebrew Passover from the Earliest Times to A.D. 70* [London, 1963], p. 267) describes the biblical Passover meal emphasizing the importance of blood. Cf. Plate 3.

The first plague which struck Egypt was that of blood:

> "Take your staff and stretch out your hand over the waters of Egypt, over the rivers and their canals, their marshland, and all their reservoirs, and let them turn to blood throughout the land of Egypt down to the contents of every tub or jar." Moses and Aaron did as Yahweh commanded. He raised his staff and in the sight of Pharaoh and his court he struck the waters of the river and all the water in the river changed to blood. (Exodus 7:19-20)

Midrashic literature greatly elaborates upon the role of blood.[36] From the above we may also note the double nature of the Passover blood — maleficent to the Egyptians but beneficent to the Israelites.

But what of the lance? For a textual allusion to such an instrument, we have only to consult the liturgy of the evening where we find a single passage uniting both a lance and blood:

ויוציאנו ה׳ ממצרים ביד חזקה ובזרע נטויה ובמרא גדל ובאתות ובמפתים
(דברים כ״ו ח׳): ... ובזרע נטויה. זו החרב... ובמפתים, זה הדם.[37]

> "And the Eternal brought us forth out of Egypt with a mighty hand and with outstretched arm and with great awe and with signs and with wonders." (Deut. 26:8).... "With an outstretched arm": this refers to the sword.... "And with wonders": this refers to the plague of blood.

---

[36] For example *The Midrash Shemot Rabbah* מדרש רבה על חמישה חומשי תורה וחמש מגילות מתנות כהונא ואסיפת אמרי Vol. 2 [Jerusalem, 1965] 9:9-11) comments:

נטה ידך ... ואפילו מה שהמצרי רוקק דם הוא.

" 'Stretch out your hand' (Exodus 7:19): Even the spittle of the Egyptians was [turned to] blood." It continues explaining that even the Egyptian idols were stricken. The Midrashim *Psikta Rabbati, Tanḥuma Beḥadash Ubeyashan, Vayosha* and *Psikta de Rab Kahani* further develop the theme (see Louis Ginzberg, *The Legends of the Jews* [Philadelphia, 1938], II, 342-349). According to one *Haggadah* MS fragment the entire Redemption is attributable to blood:

מארץ ארורים גאלתנו בזכות דם פסח ודם ברית אבות.

"You redeemed us from an accursed land because of the merits of the blood of the Paschal sacrifice and the blood of the covenant of our fathers" (I. Abrahams, "Some Egyptian Fragments of the Passover Haggadah," Jewish Quarterly Review, X [1898], 46-47).

But of greater importance to us is the use of an actual *lance-qui-saigne* in the *Seder* ritual of the Syrian Jewish community of Brooklyn. At the beginning of the *Seder* the head of the household (the officiant) takes a knife, dips it into wine and then bisects a portion of unleavened bread (*matzah*) with it.[38] Evidence gathered by Mendel Metzger in his doctoral dissertation on illuminated *Haggadah* manuscripts[39] tends to indicate that the use of such an instrument for fulfilling the ritually prescribed gesture of breaking the *matzah*, may have been quite common during the Middle Ages. A knife is often ostensibly present in the illuminations of the *Seder* table contained in medieval Haggadah manuscripts. It is the *only* piece of silverwear depicted and it is *always* found in the presence of wine, or a cup or decanter presumably containing this ritually prescribed beverage.

In an illumination of a *Seder* scene contained in a late thirteenth-century *Haggadah* of the Spanish rite (British Museum Or. 2737, folio 91 recto)[40] the following objects are to be found on the table:

> Une cruche, la matsa, une coupe, une carafe, un couteau et une corbeille tressée dont le contenu n'est pas clairement visible.[41]

Three men are behind this table. One of them holds a knife:

> La figure de droite tient un couteau; peut-être est-ce pour nous indiquer que selon le rite elle va couper la matsa.[42]

---

[37] *La Haggada commentée*, pp. 32-34. Lehrman, notes that "pour certains commentateurs 'l'épée' dans la Hagada désigne effectivement la mort par l'épée: d'après une tradition lorsque les premiers nés apprirent ce qui les menaçait, ils demandèrent à leurs parents de laisser partir les Israélites, mais ils rencontrèrent un refus absolu. Alors les premiers-nés s'avancèrent, l'épée à la main et tuèrent de nombreux Egyptiens" (*Ibid.*, p. 34).

[38] On the *Seder* plate are three *matzot*. The practice of breaking in two the middle piece of *matzah*, is standard. What is unique here, is the use of a knife for this purpose.

[39] See note 12.

[40] Reproduced as Plate XII, fig. 54 in Metzger's thesis and in his book. Cf. the description of this MS in G. Margoliouth, *Catalogue of the Hebrew and Samaritan Manuscripts in the British Museum* (London, 1965), II, 203 entry 609.

[41] Metzger, "La Haggada enluminée," thesis, pp. 100-101. Cf. *La Haggada enluminée*, I: *Etude iconographique*... (Leiden, 1973), pp. 81-82.

[42] Metzger, *Ibid.*

Two are in a reclining position:

> De plus les deux figures de droite et de gauche s'appuient visiblement sur de petits coussins clairs qu'on aperçoit dans les angles formés par la table et le cadre décoratif. Ce détail montre le souci qu'eut l'artiste d'indiquer un élément qui est caractéristique de la réunion de la table du *séder*.[43]

An illumination contained in another early fourteenth-century Spanish rite *Haggadah* (Ryl. Hebrew MS 6, fol. 19 verso) depicts a man raising a cup in his right hand and a smaller figure pouring wine. "Sur la table couverte d'une nappe blanche, on voit d'ailleurs une autre carafe et une coupe, des matsot et un *couteau*."[44] In the Sarajevo *Haggadah* (fourteenth century) there is a scene of a family *Seder* in which one figure appears to be cutting a piece of *matzah* with a knife. Two whole *matzot* are on the table.[45] Note that in the ritual three *matzot* must be contained on the *kearah*. The middle one only is to be broken.

Similarly a knife lies near a glass or a wine flask in several Ashkenazic *Haggadot* of the second half of the fifteenth century for example: Rossi 958 of Parma, Biblioteca Palatina MS Parma 3143 [fols 3 recto, 4 recto, and 11 verso],[46] and the Cincinnati *Haggadah*

---

[43] Metzger, *Ibid.*
[44] Metzger, "La Haggada enluminée," thesis, pp. 98-99. Cf. *La Haggada enluminée*, I: *Etude iconographique* ... (Leiden, 1973), pp. 80-81. Italics mine.
[45] See Plate 2 in our study.
[46] Metzger describes these three illuminations respectively in the following manner:

> On voit une partie de la table couverte d'une nappe et posés dessus, une carafe de vin, un verre et une *matsa* ainsi qu'un couteau (*La Haggada enluminée*, I: *Etude iconographique* ... [Leiden, 1973], p. 97 and Plate XVII, fig. 79).
> On voit une représentation d'un intérieur plus simple une pièce à petite fenêtre quadrillée d'où pend une lampe à truite.... Sur trois côtés d'une table se tiennent trois personnages. La table est couverte d'une nape bordée de franges. Sur la table sont posés trois verres, deux couteaux et des *matsot* (*Ibid.*, p. 115; Plate XX, fig. 98).
> Ainsi dans le cod. de Rossi 958 on voit une femme debout derrière l'homme qui est assis à la table du *séder*; celui-ci tient apparemment deux *matsot* ... sur la table sont posés un plat, un verre et un couteau ... l'enlumineur a suspendu au dessus de la table une lampe à huile à six branches (*Ibid.*, p. 194 and Plate XLII, fig. 240).

[folio 2, verso].[47] The presence of such an instrument in *so many* illuminations must no doubt indicate that it possessed ritual significance; and it is not at all difficult to see a resemblance between the bleeding lance and the ceremonial knife dipped in wine.

The Candelabras

In the Grail procession a pair of candelabras follow the *lance-qui-saigne*:

> Atant dui autre vallet vindrent,
> Qui candeliers en lor mains tindrent
> De fin or, ouvrez a neel
> Li vallet estoient molt bel
> Qui les chandeliers aportoient.
> En chascun chandelier ardoient
> Dis chandeilles atot le mains. (3213-3219)

Since the appearance of such objects can be explained on pragmatic as well as on ritualistic grounds, and since Chrétien does not elaborate upon their presence, I do not feel obligated to discuss these instruments at any great length. However, since the proponents of the Byzantine Mass theory take pains to mention the presence of candles in the eucharistic procession, I would like to note that candles also play a role in the *Seder*. At the commencement of every Jewish Festival (the evening of the previous day), candles are lit in the household. This is as true of the Passover festival as of all others, and specific reference to these Passover candles may be found in medieval rabbinic texts.[48] However if the *Seder* falls on a Saturday night (the conclusion of the Jewish Sabbath) a special prayer known as *Havdalah* ("separation," i.e., of the Sabbath from the rest of the

---

[47] Franz Landsberger, "The Cincinnati Haggadah and its Decorator," *Hebrew Union College Annual*, XV (1940), 529-558, esp. Fig. 7.

[48] For example:

בבוא איש מבית מקדש מעט ומצא ... נרות דולקות (sic)....

(Hayarḥi, *Sepher Hamanhig*, p. 129, paragraph 56). "When one returns from the synagogue, he [should] find candles burning."

and

וכשיבא אדם אל ביתו ומוצא נרות דולקות (sic).

(Abudarham, p. 116)

"When one arrives at his home, he [should] find candles burning."

week) is recited over other candles. In this ceremony a boy (usually) or someone other than the officiant holds up at least two candles or wicks before the assembled *Seder* participants so that the light of the flames may be reflected upon them. Reference to this ceremony is of course explicitly made in rabbinic sources. For example *Sepher Pardes Hagadol* mentions this ceremony in two places:

ואם חל להיות במוצאי שבת מברך ... בורא מארי האש.[49]

"If [the *Seder*] falls on Saturday night one pronounces the benediction "who createst the light of the fire."

ואם חל במ"ש מברך ... נר ...[50]

"If [the *Seder*] falls on Saturday night one blesses ... the candle."

Both Hayarḥi [51] and Abudarham [52] also specifically mention this ceremony, and illustrations of it may be found in medieval *Haggadah* manuscripts. In the *Haggadah* British Museum Add. 14761, illuminations depicting this ritual are contained in the fourteenth century portion of the manuscript. [53] The first illumination is marginal: Next to the word *Havdalah* a boy holds a candle; he faces a man holding a cup in his left hand. In the second illustration, next to the initial word of the benediction over the flame, a child holds a long twisted candle while a seated man holding a cup raises his free hand to the flame. [54] In illuminated Ashkenazic *Haggadot* the *Havdalah* light takes the form of an oil lamp with multiple burners. [55]

It appears possible that the multi-candle candelabras brought in by the *vallés*, "youths," at the beginning of the *soirée* at the Fisher King's castle may have had a relationship to the multi-flame *Havdalah* lights held by a boy at the beginning of the *Seder* ceremony.

---

[49] *Sepher Pardes Hagadol*, p. 52, paragraph 132.
[50] *Sepher Pardes Hagadol*, p. 53, paragraph 133.
[51] *Sepher Hamanhig*, p. 131, paragraph 62.
[52] *Sepher Abudarham*, p. 117.
[53] Metzger ("La Haggada enluminée," thesis, p. 125; *La Haggada enluminée*, I: *Etude iconographique*... [Leiden, 1973], p. 95) informs us they are found on folios 24, verso and 26, recto. He reproduces them as Plate XVI, figs. 75 and 76 respectively. Margoliouth (*Catalogue*, p. 197, entry no. 605) notes that these pages are found within the fourteenth-century portion of the MS.
[54] Metzger, *Ibid*.
[55] "La Haggada enluminée," thesis, pp. 128-129. Cf. *La Haggada enluminée*, I: *Etude iconographique*... (Leiden, 1973), pp. 95-98.

The Meal

After the Grail procession, the Fisher King calls for water and the two wash. A table is then brought in; and a white tablecloth, which is elaborately described by Chrétien, is placed upon it:

>   Et li sire as vallés comande
>   L'eve doner et napes traire.
>   Cil le font qui le doivent faire
>   Et qui acostumé l'avoient.
>   Li sire et li vallés lavoient
>   Lor mains d'eve caude tempree.
>   Et dui vallet ont aportee
>   Une table lee d'yvoire;
>   ... ...
>   Devant lor seignor une piece
>   Et devant le vallet le tindrent,
>   Tant que dui autre vallet vindrent,
>   Qui aporterent deus eschaces.
>   ... ...
>   Sor ces eschaces fu assise
>   La table, et la nape fu mise. (3254-3261, 3264-
>   3267, 3276-3277)

In the *Seder* too, one is obligated to wash prior to the meal proper (both Hayarḥi and Abudarham take note of this practice),[56] and the *Seder* table is required to be adorned with a cloth. The Talmud specifically prescribes this:

> (*Pesaḥim*, 100b)   ואם הביא פורס מפה.

If they brought [the table], a tablecloth is to be placed upon it;

and Hayarḥi attests that this practice was still in effect at the end of the twelfth century:

> יפרוש מפה על השלחן [57]

One places a tablecloth upon the table.

---

[56] *Sepher Hamanhig*, 134, paragraph 76, and *Abudarham Hashalem* (Jerusalem, 1956), p. 232.

[57] *Sepher Hamanhig*, p. 129, paragraph 56.

Likewise medieval *Haggadah* manuscript illuminations depict a *Seder* table adorned with a cloth.[58]

A sumptuous meal is now served to the Fisher King and his guest. The foods of this meal correspond closely to the ritual foods ordained for the *Seder* banquet:

> Li premiers mes fu d'une hanche
> De cerf de craisse au poivre chaut.
> Vins clers a boire ne lor faut,
> En colpes d'or, söés a boivre.
> De la hance de cerf al poivre
> Uns vallés devant als trencha,
> Qui a lui traite la hanche a
> Atot le tailleoir d'argant,
> Et les morsiax lor met devant
> Sor un gastel qui fu entiers. (3280-3289)

The first course was thus a combination of three ingredients: a whole *gastel* plus pepper and meat carved on the *tailleoir d'argent*. Note that Chrétien is most careful to employ the word *gastel* rather than bread (*pan*). Foerster defines the former as *Kuchen* "cake" or *Kuchenscheibe* "a round piece of cake."[59] The Tobler-Lommatzsch dictionary similarly translates *gastel* by the term *Kuchen*.[60] We have seen that the supporters of the Christian theories had difficulty explaining why such a combination of foods should be carved on *the* silver platter (which, having religious significance should be reserved for ritual use exclusively). However, according to the Judaic theory that I am proposing, such details are easily accounted for.

---

[58] Metzger, "La Haggada enluminée," thesis, p. 103. Cf. *La Haggada enluminée*, I: *Etude iconographique* ... (Leiden, 1973), pp. 83-84.

[59] Wendelin Foerster, *Kristian von Troyes: Wörterbuch zu seinen sämtlichen Werken* (Halle, 1914), p. 151. N.B. in the third edition of this dictionary (Wendelin Foerster, Hermann Breuer, *Wörterbuch zu Kristian von Troyes' sämtlichen Werken*, 3rd edition [Tübingen, 1964], p. 133) the definition *Brotkissen* is also given for *gastel*. This latter meaning is based upon the variant reading *platel*. However it appears to me that this variant cannot be correct since it would be superfluous for Chrétien to then specify that this object *fu entiers*. Such a specification would of course be necessary in the case of a brittle piece of flat cake — *gastel*.

[60] Tobler-Lommatzsch, *Altfranzösisches Wörterbuch*, Vol. 4 (Wiesbaden, 1960). Tobler-Lommatzsch also takes note of the variant *platiel* or *platel* and further explains that according to Baist, *gastel* could mean *Brotfladen* ("a round, flat piece of bread") or *Brotkissen*. The primary meaning, however, is a type of cake (*Kuchen*).

During the Passover festival, one is permitted to eat only unleavened bread (*matzah*) and at the *Seder* one is *required* to partake of this food. Until this century, with the advent of mass baking machinery, such unleavened bread took the form of flat, round cakes, conforming exactly to the definitions of *gastel*. The many illustrations of *matzot* found in illuminated *Haggadah* manuscripts confirm the fact that in the Middle Ages the unleavened bread had this appearance.[61] Raphael Levy further remarks that in the Hebrew-French glossary of Joseph ben Simson (1240), the word *gatey* itself was used to translate the word *matzah* found in Exodus 12:39.[62] The second plate of the mishnaic *Seder* — corresponding to our *tailleoir d'argent* — contained a combination of *matzah* and meat;[63] and today, as in medieval times, a shank bone of lamb must adorn the *Seder* plate in commemoration of the Paschal sacrifice:

סה) ולוקח את הסל שבו שני תבשילין והם שני מיני בשר והצלי זכר לפסח
והמבושל זכר לחגיגה המבושלת.

סו) נהגו בצרפת ובפרובינצא לצלות את זרוע השה זכר לדבר ויציאנו ה'
אלהינו וגו' בזרוע נטויה.[64]

65 And one takes the basket which has two cooked species, namely two [differently prepared] types of meat. The roasted species in remembrance of the Paschal sacrifice and the cooked species in remembrance of the holiday offering that was cooked.
66 It was customary in France and Provence to roast the arm of a sheep in remembrance of the verse "And the Lord our God took us out ... with an outstretched arm."

In the *Seder*, immediately prior to partaking of the meal, one is required to make a strange sort of sandwich of *matzah* and bitter herbs while reciting:

---

[61] Metzger ("La Haggada enluminée," thesis, pp. 11, 20, 135, 143, 258, 259, 266, 272, 275) describes illuminations in which the *matzot* have the form of a disc. Cf. Plates 2 and 4 in our study. Even today round, hand-baked *matzot* may often be found on *Seder* tables.
[62] Raphael Levy, *Trésor de la langue des Juifs français au moyen âge* (Austin, 1964), p. 122.
[63] *La Haggada commentée*, p. 5.
[64] *Sepher Hamanhig*, p. 132; Cf. *Sepher Pardes Hagadol*, p. 53, paragraph 133.

זכר למקדש כהלל: כן עשה הלל בזמן שבית המקדש קים היה כורך (פסח)
מצה ומרור ואוכל ביחד לקים מה שנאמר על מצות ומרורים יאכלהו:
(במדבר ט' י"א).[65]

In remembrance of the Sanctuary according to the custom of Hillel. Thus was Hillel accostomed to do when the Sanctuary was in existence. He would put together [the Paschal lamb], unleavened bread and bitter herbs and eat them together in order to fulfill that which is said "Upon unleavened bread and bitter herbs shall they eat it." (Numbers 9.11)

Thus, reminding us of the *gastel*, meat, and condiment served to the Fisher King and to Perceval, the *Haggadah* proclaims that the first course eaten by Hillel (and by the participants of the *Seder* in a slightly modified form), is a combination of unleavened bread, meat, and bitter herbs.[66]

The fare at the Fisher King's banquet was most copious:

> Vins clers a boire ne lor faut,
> ... ...
> L'en n'aporte mie a dangier
> Les vins et les mes a la table,
> Qui sunt plaisant et delitable. (3282, 3312-3314)

The *Seder* too is considered as a repast of plenty. One of the opening prayers, the *Ha Laḥma Anya* ("This is the bread of affliction") recited

---

[65] *La Haggadah commentée*, p. 54.

[66] It is interesting to note that the principal *Seder* dish among the Tunisian Jews is called "Muski" and is comprised of *matzot*, lamb and vegetables. See Mordekhai Satbon and Avraham Tal, "Miminhagei Yahadut Tunisia," *Yalkut Minhagim*, p. 145.

The fact that at Chrétien's meal a haunch of *cerf* is eaten rather than the leg of lamb (*agnel*) of the Seder, might easily be accounted for in that Chrétien is transposing this ritual meal into the setting of a courtly romance. Meat from a hunt would be the only dish for nobility such "meat was obtained almost exclusively from the chase" (E. R. Chamberlin, *Life in Medieval France, European Life Series,* ed. Peter Quennell [London, 1967], p. 151). Among such meat venison figured prominently. *Agnel* was not to be found. *Le Ménagier de Paris* (La Société de Bibliophiles français, *Le Ménagier de Paris, traité de morale et d'économie domestique composé vers 1393 par un Parisien* [Paris, 1846], II) only mentions *mouton* on one occasion (p. 98). *Agnel* is not even listed — in contrast to numerous listings of such meats as *porc, jambon, cerf* and *bœuf*. Similarly Tobler-Lommatzsch, Wartburg, and Godefroy never refer to *agnel* in the context of a hunt. By contrast they cite many examples of *cerf* in this context.

in Aramaic and repeated in French at the time of Chrétien, invites all who are hungry to partake of the *Seder* meal:

כל דכפין ייתי ויכל.
כל דצריך ייתי ויפסח.[67]

Whoever is hungry may he come and eat.
Whoever is in need, may he come and celebrate Passover with us.

Just as Chrétien stresses the fact that wines were served at the Fisher King's table, so too at the *Seder* table is the drinking of wine obligatory:

> Cette obligation est telle que la Michna qui en parle (Pessa'him X, 1) précise que le pauvre doit recevoir de la caisse de bienfaisance de quoi les aquérir.... Le Midrache voit une allusion à ces quatre coupes de Pessa'h dans le récit biblique du maître-échanson de Pharaon: le mot כוס, coupe, y figure à quatre reprises.... Pour Rabbi Josué ben Lévy les quatre coupes sont le symbole de quatre coupes d'ivresse que le Saint, béni-soit-il, fera boire aux Nations.... L'Explication de Rav Houna est la plus connue: les quatre coupes correspondent aux quatre expressions de la délivrance.... (Exode VI, 6-8).[68]

The Mishnah explains:

מצוה על אדם לשמח בניו ובני ביתו במה משמחו ביין שנ' ויין ישמח לבב אנוש ר' יהודה אומר הנשים בראוי להם (sic) והקטנים בראוי להם.[69]

It is obligatory upon a man to cause his children and the members of his household to rejoice. By what means does one cause someone to rejoice? By wine, as it is written "Wine gladdens the heart of man." Rabbi Yehudah said "One gives to women a portion which is appropriate to them and to children a portion which is appropriate to them."

Chrétien does not describe in detail the foods served at the meal; all that he states is that the repast was fit for a king, a count, or an

---

[67] *La Haggada commentée*, pp. 2-3.
[68] *La Haggada commentée*, pp. 2-3.
[69] *Pesaḥim*, X, 4.

emperor (vv. 3316-3317). He does make specific mention, however, of the fruits served:

> Dates, figues et nois muscades
> Et girofle et pomes grenades
> Et laituaires en la fin
> Et gigembras alexandrin,
> Or pleuris et arcoticum,
> Resontif et stomaticum. (3325-3330) [70]

According to Godefroy, *laituaire* signifies "confiture épaisse faite avec des prunes, des poires, raisiné, marmelade." [71]

One of the symbolic foods at the *Seder* is the *ḥaroset*, a brownish paste of apples, pomegranates, almonds and cinnamon mixed in red wine. This mixture is meant to recall the mortar, bricks, and clay which Pharaoh demanded of his slaves. [72] In medieval times the recipe resembled even more closely the ingredients described by Chrétien.

Rashi explains:

וחרוסת מצוה מאי מצוה זכר לתפוח שנאמ' תחת התפוח עוררתיך. ויש אומרים זכר לתפוח כשהיו נושאים הטיט על צוארם היה טופח הטיט על צוארם ונעשה מוגליא לכך משימין בו מיני פירות שדכו במדורה. תבלין זכר לתבן ולכך אנו אוכלין הירקות שהם כמין תבן. ור' א"ר יוחנן זכר לטיט והילכך בעי לאקהווי וצריך לעשותו כעין טיט ותניא כוותיה דר' יוחנן תבלין זכר לתבן כגון קנמון וזנגבייל שדומין לתבן חרוסת זכר לטיט. [73]

And *ḥaroset* is a precept in remembrance of the apple tree [*tapuaḥ*] as it is written "I awakened you under the apple tree" (Song of Songs 8:5). Some are of the opinion that it is in remembrance of the swelling (*tipuaḥ*), for when [the Israelites] carried the clay upon their necks, the clay would swell upon their necks and form a pustule.

---

[70] The exact translation of vv. 3329-3330 is not known. Hilka in his notes (pp. 690-691) says that these dishes which were types of electuaries had medicinal properties.

[71] Frédéric Godefroy, *Dictionnaire de l'ancienne langue française du XI⁰ au XV⁰ siècle* (Paris, 1881-1885). Cf. Tobler-Lommatzsch which defines *leitüaire* as *Latwerge*, "electuary."

[72] "Le plat du Sédere," *La Haggada commentée*, the beginning. Rabbi David Berdah's *Haggada de Pâque* (p. 9) similarly describes the *ḥaroset* as containing dates, almonds, pomegranates, etc.

[73] *Sepher Pardes Hagadol*, p. 55, paragraph 135.

For this reason we include in it [the *ḥaroset*] various types of fruit that are crushed with a mortar. Spices are in remembrance of the straw [used in the manufacture of the bricks] (and this is the very reason we also eat greens because they are a type of straw). And Rabbi Yoḥanan said *ḥaroset* is in remembrance of the clay and therefore we make it loose and cause it to appear like clay. We learned in accordance with Rabbi Yoḥanan that in remembrance of the straw we need spices like cinnamon and *zingebal* (*zizembral*, "an Arabian spice, probably ginger" — Jastrow). *Ḥaroset* is in remembrance of the clay.

Abudarham's recipe for *ḥaroset* is as follows:

וחרוסת היא מצוה מדברי סופרים זכר לטיט שהיו ישראל משועבדין בו במצרים. ועושין אותה ממיני פירות מתוקים ומרורים וחומץ ומתבלין אותם בתבלין לדמותם לטיט שיש בו מכל דבר וצריך שתהיה עבה כמו הטיט זכר לטיט כמו שאמרנו וישים בה מיני קיהוי כגון תפוחים חמוצים זכר לתחת התפוח עוררתיך (שיר השירים ח׳, ה). ואגוזים לזכר אל גנת אגוז ירדתי (שם ו׳, י״א) ותאנים זכר להתאנה חנטה פגיה (שם ב׳, י״ג) ותבלין כגון קנה וקנמון שהיא קצבה אל דריכה וסנבל שדומין לתבן שהיו מגבלין בו הטיט במצרים.[74]

And *ḥaroset* is a precept of the Scribes in remembrance of the clay that the Israelites were forced to work with in Egypt. And it is made from types of sweet and sour fruits and vinegar. And these are seasoned with spices to give them the appearance of clay which has in it all sorts of things. And it must be thick like clay in remembrance of the clay, as I have stated. And sour ingredients are placed in it as for example sour apples in remembrance of the verse "I awakened you under the apple tree" (Song of Songs 8:5); and nuts, in remembrance of the verse "I went down to the nut orchard" (*Ibid.*, 6:11); and figs, in remembrance of the verse "The fig tree is forming its first figs" (*Ibid.*, 2:13); and spices like calamus (or sugar cane according to the Ben Yehuda *Thesaurus*) and cinnamon, which is *kaṣbah aldariyka* [in Arabic] (قصبة الدريكة ; N.B. *Kaṣba(ah)* is defined as "cane" or "sugarcane" by Dozy) and *sunbul* (سنبل "spikenard," Dozy, Wehr) which are similar in appearance to straw which they [the Israelites] used to mix into the clay, in Egypt.

The late thirteenth-century Sephardic *Haggadah* British Museum Or. 2737 (fol. 88, verso) depicts the preparation of this dish:

---

[74] *Sepher Abudarham*, p. 117.

l'enluminure montre deux hommes assis, l'un en face de l'autre, sur des coussins posés à terre, les jambes bien écartées de part et d'autre et d'un grand mortier auquel ils s'appuient d'une main. De l'autre ils manient des pilons, d'un mouvement alterné, si l'on en juge d'après les positions respectives de ceux-ci. Ils sont en train de broyer les ingredients dont le mélange constitue le [sic] *'harosset*: noix, pommes, figues, dattes, canelle, le tout mélangé à du vin. Cette scène est accompagnée d'une inscription en hébreu qui dit: *élou ossin 'harosset* (ceux-là font *le* [sic] *'harosset*). [75]

While the fifteenth-century Ashkenazic *Haggadah* Nuremberg II contains an illumination similarly depicting the manufacture of ḥaroset which Müller-Schlosser describes in the following manner:

> Zwei Knaben bereiten die süsse Speise (*ḥarosset*); einer schalt Feigen, Aepfel, Birnen, Nüsse, der andere stampft sie in einem Mörser. [76]

Returning to Chrétien's narrative we may recall that on several occasions during the meal at the Fisher King's castle, the grail reappears:

> Et li graals endementiers
> Par devant als retrespassa,
> ... ...
> Qu'a chascun mes que l'on servoit,
> Par devant lui trespasser voit
> Le graal trestot descovert. (3290-3291, 3299-3301)

Because of the grail's reappearance with each new course, some scholars have advanced the claim that the grail miraculously produced all of the abundant foods served at the banquet. Unfortunately, Chrétien's text cannot justify such an inference — simultaneity does not imply causality. It also appears most unlikely to imagine, as some have done, that, commencing with its second appearance, the grail was transformed into a magical instrument capable of passing through the room by itself. If the grail so passes, it is because someone carries

---

[75] Metzger, "La Haggada enluminée," thesis, p. 56. Cf. *La Haggada enluminée I: Etude iconographique...* (Leiden, 1973), p. 57 and Plate VII, fig. 26.

[76] Metzger, "La Haggada enluminée," thesis, p. 56. Cf. *La Haggada enluminée I: Etude iconographique...* (Leiden, 1973), p. 58. Cf. Müller-Schlosser, p. 131.

it. No doubt Chrétien chose not to describe the Grail Bearer repeatedly, in order not to detract from the importance of the grail and of Perceval's thoughts. Though the controversy over whether the words *trestot descovert* mean "unveiled" (the adherents of the Christian thesis) or "very apparent" (Frappier) does seem legitimate, neither interpretation presents any difficulty to one who adopts the Judaic theory since on several different occasions during the *Seder* ceremony one is required to cover and then to uncover the *kearah* (with the *matzot*) *and* to show it to all present. [77]

The following directions contained in a *Haggadah* fragment of the Cairo genizah demonstrate that this practice of showing the *Seder* plate to those present is indeed a very old one:

תם יחרק אל מאידה תלת מראד (מראה) ויקול הא השתא הכא.

then one moves the table (plate) three times and says "now we are here...." [78]

Following the meal at the Fisher King's castle, wines are served ("Piument ou n'ot ne miel ne poivre, / Et viez moré et cler syrop" [vv. 3332-3333]). Then Perceval and his host both go to sleep.

---

[77] See, for example, the following directions in *La Haggada commentée*:

> p. 7. On découvre les *Matsot* et l'on soulève le plat en récitant "voici le pain de misère."
> p. 11. On découvre les *Matsot*, et le chef de famille répond par le récit de la Sortie d'Egypte.
> p. 25. On couvre les *Matsot* et on lève la coupe.
> p. 26. On pose la coupe et l'on découvre les *Matsot*.
> p. 44. On montre le pain azyme aux assistants: cette *Matsa* (ce pain azyme) pourquoi la mangeons nous? Parce que la pâte de nos pères n'avait pas eu le temps de lever etc.
> p. 45. On montre les herbes amères aux assistants.
> p. 46. On couvre les *Matsot*: on lève la coupe et l'on dit à haute voix: c'est pourquoi il est de notre devoir de remercier. On pose la coupe et découvre les pains azymes.
> p. 49. On recouvre la *Matsa*, on lève la coupe et l'on dit Béni sois-Tu.

[78] I. Abrahams, "Some Egyptian fragments of the Passover Hagada," *Jewish Quarterly Review*, X (1898), 50. See also notes of Messrs. David Kaufman and W. Bacher (*JQR*, X, 380 and 382-383 respectively). The Arabic transcription of the above is the following:

ثمّ يحرك المائدة ثلث مراة ويقول

Perhaps corresponding to these three movements of the plate are the three times the grail's appearances are mentioned in Chrétien's text.

Similarly in the *Seder* two cups of wine are to be imbibed after the conclusion of the meal and nothing further is to be eaten until bedtime.[79]

---

[79] Underlying this set of basic parallels between Chrétien de Troyes's Grail Banquet and the Passover *Seder*, are a series of less rigorous similarities. While such motifs found in Chrétien's description may very well be completely unintentional on his part, they do however conform to the general context of the Passover ceremony. I present them here in the order of Chrétien's narrative with the sole intention of adding background color to my exposé rather than with the insistence that each detail be accepted as an inviolable proof of my theory of Judaic origin.

When Perceval enters the main hall of the Grail Castle, the entire room is inundated with candlelight (3187-3189). As I have already mentioned in passing, this description conforms to the directives of Hayarḥi and Abudarham that candles must be burning when one enters the home to begin the Passover *Seder* (See above, note 48). We are later informed that the Fisher King cannot move by himself because he had suffered a wound through both thighs (3342-3343; 3507-3515).

Though the *celtisants* who attempt to relate this character to such maimed gods as Nuadu and Bran do present some interesting parallels, we should also note that many philologists believe that the very word for Passover, in Hebrew, *Pesaḥ*, is derived from a triliteral root meaning "to limp." This root is used, for example, in I Kings 18:26 to describe the dance performed about the alter of Bal: *Vayepashu al hamizbeaḥ asher asah,* "And they danced bending the knee before the altar which they had made." The execution of a "limping dance" is an integral part of certain present-day as well as ancient Near-Eastern rites (T. H. Gaster, *Passover: Its History and Tradition* [New York, 1949] p. 23). Such dances were performed by the sailors of Tyre in the beginning of the Christian Era and by Pre-Islamic Arabs. The theory has thus been advanced that the primitive Passover ceremony contained a similar "limping ritual" executed as part of a springtime rite. Professor Holmes has attempted to show that a relationship exists between the maimed Fisher King and Jacob, who in Genesis 32:66-32 fought with an angel and was wounded in the thigh (*Chrétien, Troyes, and the Grail*, pp. 102-103). We shall have more to say about this interpretation in Chapter Five.

When Perceval enters the Grail Castle the Fisher King asks his young visitor questions concerning his journey and the youth replies to his queries:

> Et li preudom li dist: "Amis
> De quel part venistes vos hui?"
> — "Sire, fait il, hui matin mui
> De Biaurepaire, issi a non."
> — Si m'aït Diex, fait li preudom,
> Trop grant jornee avez hui faite:
> Vos meüstes ainz que la gaite
> Eüst hui matin l'aube cornee."
> — "Ainz estoit ja prime sonee,
> Fait li vallés, jel vos affi." (3120-3128)

No doubt any host would ask such questions of an arriving guest. However, in the *Seder* of numerous Sephardic communities, the officiant asks the

Part Two

Contact between the Jews of Spain and France and Relations between Jew and Christian in Northern France

The Hebraic thesis carries with it the advantage of easily explaining how Chrétien could have been acquainted with this ritual. Though most of the basic similarities between the Passover meal and Chrétien's narrative exist in the talmudic account of the *Seder* [80]

---

youngest present a set of preliminary questions so as to dramatize the significance of the Exodus. In this ritual, which is conducted either before or at the beginning of the *Seder* service, a youngster enters the room disguised as a traveler. A dialogue similar to the following one conducted by the Babylonian Jews (which I translate from the Hebrew transcription of A. Ben-Yaakov, *Yalkut Minhagim*, p. 33) takes place between the master of the house (the father) and the young "arrival":

>   FATHER: From where have you come?
>   SON: From Egypt.
>   FATHER: And where are you going?
>   SON: To Jerusalem.
>   FATHER: And where are your provisions for the journey?

Following this exchange, the traditional questions are elicited from the youngest present.

An almost identical set of questions may be found among the Khurdistani Jews (Yitzhak Amadi, "Miminhagei Yahadut Kurdistan," *Yalkut Minhagim*, p. 61) and among Libyan Jews (see F. Zuarts, *Ibid.*, p. 87). Similarly, the Jews of Persia (E. Ben-Ezra, "Minhagei Hasedarim" *Hadoar* [Nisan 5711- April 1951], p. 471; R. M. Weinberger, "Pesah im Yehudei Paras," *Hadoar* [Nisan 5707 - April 1947]), of Morocco (Shalom Danino, "Miminhagei Yahadut Maroko," *Yalkut Minhagim*, p. 110) and Baghdad (*Seder Haggadah shel Pesah im Srah Aravi Vitargum Aravi, Minhag K"K Bagdad* [Leghorn, 1867], folio 9b, paragraph 3; Cf. A. Ben-Yaakov, *Hagilgal* I [5704, 1904], 19) practice this ritual as do the Syrian Jews.

[80] Leaning (*Pesahim*, 108a)
Dividing the *matzah*, candles (102b)
Removing the table [plate] (115b)
Questions (109; *Mishnah* X:4 [115b])
Bringing in the table (100b)
Spreading the table-cloth (100a, 100b)
Washing the hands (115b)
Unleavened bread, Paschal haunch, bitter herbs (*Mishnah* X:5 [116a, 116b])
Wine (*Mishnah* X:1 [99b], X:2 [114a]; *Gemara* X passim, esp. 108a, 108b, 109a)

as well as in the *Seder* as practiced by the Jews of Troyes,[81] we have seen that the resemblances between the Grail banquet and the *Seder* of the Sephardic Jews are particularly striking. I should therefore like to suggest that Chrétien had either direct or indirect knowledge of the latter *Seder* ritual. The probability of such an occurrence seems quite likely if we recall that there was both widespread economic and religious contact between the Jews of Troyes and their coreligionists in Europe and the Levant and that channels of communication existed between Jew and Christian. Chrétien may therefore have acquired knowledge of the Sephardic form of the *Seder* directly or indirectly from Jews coming from Spain (we shall consider below the routes of Spain-Troyes and Spain-Narbonne-Troyes) or *possibly* from the Orient. It is not necessary to postulate the apostasy of Chrétien[82] (though conversions did occur[83]) in order to propose a Jewish influence upon his work. Jews had commercial dealings with the lords of Champagne. There was also a lively exchange of ideas between Jew and Gentile at Troyes. It is known that Count Henry consulted with Jews on knotty problems of the Old Testament.[84] Before analyzing these channels of cultural transmission, let us quickly glance at the situation of the Jews of Troyes.

The Jewish community of Troyes was small but well-established. Financial documents from the first half of the eleventh century de-

---

Haroset (*Mishnah* X:3 and *Gamara* 116a)
The possibility of Chrétien's direct or indirect knowledge of this source, should not be ruled out.

[81] The rite of the Jews of Troyes closely resembled in many ways that of the Sephardim, with the important difference being that the former would not have the plate taken into a different room but rather would place it at the edge of the table (see Rashi, *Sepher Pardes Hagadol*, Rashbam on *Pesaḥim* 115b, Tosphos on *Pesaḥim* 115b, and Simḥah ben Shemuel de Vitry, *Maḥzor Vitry*, ed. Shimon Halevi Horowitz [Jerusalem, 1963], p. 283).

[82] See Holmes (*ibid.*, passim) and Jean Frappier, "Le 'Conte du Graal,' est-il une allégorie Judeo-Chrétienne?" *Romance Philology*, XVI (1962), 179-213 and XX (1966), 173-197, for two divergent views on the question.

[83] Holmes, *Chrétien, Troyes, and the Grail*, p. 52. Cf. Beryl Smalley, *The Study of the Bible in the Middle Ages*, 2nd ed. (New York, 1952), p. 157.

[84] Holmes, *Chrétien, Troyes, and the Grail*, p. 13. For accounts of friendly contacts between Christian and Jewish scholars including Stephen Harding, abbot of Cîteaux, Sigebert of Gembloux, Nicolas Manjacoria of Trois Fontaines, and the Victorines, see Smalley, *The Study of the Bible in the Middle Ages*, 2nd ed., pp. 77-197.

monstrate that the Jews there cultivated grapes and owned property.[85] They were bankers for the counts, *fermiers des péages, des impôts* as well as collectors of all sorts of revenues[86] By the beginning of the thirteenth century both lords and ecclesiastical officials did not hesitate to borrow from them.[87]

But for the Jews, Troyes's real fame resided in their Academy. In 1070 the most well-known talmudic and biblical commentator of all times, Rashi (1040-1105), founded a rabbinical academy at Troyes.[88] This scholar's influence was so great that it extended even into Christendom affecting such figures as Hugo, Richard and Andrew of Saint-Victor, Peter Comestor, Herbert of Bosham, Langton, and Nicholas of Lyra.[89] Rashi's students were in demand as rabbis and teachers even by the Jewish communities of Spain.[90] Among his students were such noted scholars as Simḥa ben Shemuel de Vitry, Yehudah ben Natan (the "Raiban"), Shemaya, Yoseph ben Shimeon Kara, Shemuel ben Meir (the "Rashbam" 1085-1158, who inherited the professorship of the Academy) and Yaakov ben Meir ("Rabbeinu Tam" 1100-1171). Other generations of rabbis succeeded these illustrious ones, and despite a most tragic auto-da-fé in 1288,[91] documents testify to the presence in Troyes of learned Jews as late as the year 1382.[92]

Let us now examine the following means by which Jews and Gentiles of Troyes may have come into contact with Sephardim: fairs, synods, the spread of schools of learning, itinerant scholars, epistles (Responsa), traveling preachers, and migrations.

---

[85] Gross, *Gallia Judaica*, p. 225.
[86] Holmes, *Chrétien, Troyes and the Grail*, pp. 12-13.
[87] Gross, *Gallia Judaica*, p. 225.
[88] Maurice Liber, *Rashi*, tr. Adele Szold (Philadelphia, 1906), p. 57.
[89] Beryl Smalley, *The Study of the Bible in the Middle Ages*, 2nd ed., pp. 77-196, 234-242. Israel Tabak, "Rashi and the Non-Jewish World," *Rashi: His Teachings and Personality*, ed. Simon Federbush (New York, 1958), pp. 107-111.
[90] Rufus Learsi [Israel Goldberg], *Israel: A History of the Jewish People* (Cleveland, 1949), p. 270.
[91] See Arsène Darmesteter, "L'autodafé de Troyes de 1288," *Revue des Etudes Juives*, II (1881), p. 199; "L'Autodafé de Troyes (24 Avril 1288)," *Arsène Darmesteter: Reliques Scientifiques recueillies par son frère* (Paris, 1890), I, 217-264; "Deux élégies du Vatican," *Ibid.*, pp. 265-308; and *Romania*, III (1874), 443-486. See also C. Lehrmann, *L'Elément juif dans la littérature française*, Collection: Présences du judaisme (Paris, 1960), I, 39-42.
[92] See Gross, *Gallia Judaica*, pp. 224-243, for a fuller listing of famous Jewish personages of Troyes.

Fairs

Troyes was an important medieval economic center. Two major fairs the *Foire chaude* (early July to September 3) and the *Foire froide* (November 2 to January 2), "attracted merchants and bankers from all of Western Europe and even from the Eastern Mediterranean." [93] *Among* those areas represented were Barcelona, Castile, Aragon, Portugal, Acre, Cyprus and occasionally Greece, Egypt and Tunis. [94]

Since Jewish merchants from many different regions played a large role in these fairs, [95] it was possible for the Jews of Northern France to meet their coreligionists from Spain, Provence and the Orient, on these occasions.

Synods

As many of the learned talmudists engaged in trade and banking, rabbinical synods were scheduled to coincide with the fairs of Troyes, when Jewish leaders would be present for commercial reasons. [96] Decisions of these synods, which bore the geographic origins of the rabbis who promulgated them, demonstrate that there was extensive contact between the Jews of northern and southern France. One such decision promulgated by an important synod of 150 French and German rabbis, under the presidency of the brothers Shemuel and Yaakov ben Meir (1085-1158 and 1100-1171, respectively), Eliezer ben Natan of Mainz and Eliezer ben Shimshon of Köln, begins as follows:

באלה התקנות נועצו והסכימו וחתמו כל זקני טרייש וחכמיה וכל סביבותיה
וגדולי אליורא וחכמי גבול ריינש ורבותינו שבפריש ושכניהם וחכמי יועצי
ליאון וקרפנטרא ולומברדיאה וחבל הים ואניוב ופייטיו וגדולי לותיר. [97]

---

[93] Holmes, *Chrétien, Troyes, and the Grail*, p. 9.
[94] Holmes (*Chrétien, Troyes and the Grail*, p. 13) cites the following list of regions represented at the fairs of Troyes:

> all parts of France, Genoa, Lucca, Bologna, Florence, Rome, Cremona, Milan, Pistoia, Asti, Siena, Piacenza, Parma, Naples, Venice, Urbino, the Low Countries, Hainaut, Brabant, Germany, Switzerland, Savoy, Pamplona, Lerida, Barcelona, Castile, Aragon, Portugal, Sweden, Acre, Cyprus and occasionally from Greece, Egypt and Tunis....

[95] Gross, *Gallia Judaica*, p. 237; Liber, *Rashi*, p. 36.
[96] Holmes, *Chrétien, Troyes, and the Grail*, p. 13.
[97] Gross, *Gallia Judaica*, pp. 232-233.

These ordinances were examined and adopted by the elders and sages of Troyes and the surrounding area, by the great men of *Elyura*, the sages of the Rhine region, our rabbis of Paris and their neighbors, the sages of Lyons and Carpentras, of Lombardy of the sea coast, of Anjou, of Poitou, and by the great men of Lorraine.

The Second Great Synod renewed a decision made by the rabbinical college of Narbonne. This decision contains the following list of participants:

יושבי צרפת אניוב פוייטוב גרמנדיא גדולי גרבונא יושבי טרוייש ודיגון אניוב פוייטו נורמדיאה ויושביהם.[98]

The inhabitants of France, Anjou, Poitou, Normandy, the great men of Narbonne, the inhabitants of Troyes and Dijon, Anjou, Poitou, Normandy and their inhabitants.

The Spread of Schools of Learning

The spread of schools of learning from Provence to northern France had already taken place before Rashi, and continued to occur after him. Learsi writes:

> From Provence... the study of the Talmud spread northward to the Rhine. Legend has it that it was brought to Narbonne by Nathan ben Isaac, one of the four emissaries from Sura; and Judah ben Meir, better known as Leontin, the first important teacher of the academy in Narbonne of whom we have definite knowledge may have been one of Nathan's pupils. [99]

Gross notes that Leontin lived in France or perhaps Lorraine and that he addressed a letter to the community of Troyes which demonstrated that he had knowledge of the internal affairs of that community. [100]

Gershom ben Yehudah (969-1038), who had either been born in France or had lived there in his youth was a pupil of Leontin and

---

[98] Gross, *Gallia Judaica*, pp. 235-236.
[99] Learsi, *Israel*, p. 268.
[100] Gross, *Gallia Judaica*, p. 300.

established a school in Mainz on the Rhine.[101] Students flocked to Gershom's school from France, Germany and Italy. A generation later Rashi himself studied in Worms, Mainz (where the commentaries of Rabbi Gershom were compiled), and Speyer, before returning to Troyes to found his own academy.

The Jews of France were also familiar with the ideas of Spanish schools of thought. D. S. Blondheim confirms that there is a close connection between the biblical glossaries of French Jews and the biblical translations of Spanish Jews,[102] and H. Gross reminds us that Rabbeinu Tam in his work *Sepher Hahakhraot (The Book of Judgments)* defends the Spanish grammarian Menahem ben Saruk against Dunash ben Labrat.[103]

Traveling Scholars

Related to the actual transmission of schools of thought is the intercourse between Jewish scholars from Spain, Provence, the Orient, and Northern France. Let us briefly examine the following paths of such communication: Spain-Troyes and Spain-Narbonne-Troyes.[104]

---

[101] Gross, *Gallia Judaica*, p. 300; Learsi, *Israel*, p. 268.

[102] D. S. Blondeim, *Contribution à la lexicographie française d'après des sources rabbiniques. Doctoral Dissertation, The Johns Hopkins University, June, 1910* (Paris, 1910), p. 4. N.B. The text of this volume was first published in *Romania* XXXIX (1910).

[103] Gross, *Gallia Judaica*, p. 231.

[104] We should not rule out the possibility of transmission from Spain through Italy to Northern France. As we have seen, Italian cities were represented at the fairs and rabbinical synods of Troyes. Even before the 1492 expulsion, Jews had come from Spain to Tuscany; and from Africa about 1,500 families had come to Palermo and 200 families to Messina. Important colonies of Jews had migrated from the Orient to Venice. Frederick II, the last of the Hohenstaufens, employed Jews to translate from the Arabic, philosophical and astronomical treatises. Among these writers were Yehudah Kohen of Toledo, later of Tuscany, and Yaakov Anatoli of Provence [Vittore Castiglioni, "Italy," *The Jewish Encyclopedia*, VII, 2; cf. Gross, op. cit., p. 374].

The works of Maimonides were studied by Italian Jews such as Hillel of Verona (1220-1295), Shabbetai ben Shelomoh of Rome and Zerahiah Hen of Barcelona who migrated to Rome and contributed much to spread the knowledge of his works. Among other devotees of their theories was Immanual ben Shelomoh of Rome, Dante's friend (Castiglioni, *op. cit.*).

Spain-Northern France

(1) Avraham ibn Ezra, the great Spanish Jewish poet and biblical exegete (1092-167), traveled as far east as Babylonia and as far west as London, sojourning in many lands. In the course of his travels, he met David ben Yoseph at Narbonne (1139),[105] and Rabbeinu Tam at Troyes:[106] "Quand Abraham ibn Ezra traversa la France," writes Gross, "il [Rabbeinu Tam] lui adressa quelques vers flatteurs, et Ibn Ezra s'écria avec surprise: 'Qui donc a fait pénétrer les Français dans le temple de la poésie?' "[107]

(2) Avraham ben Natan Hayarḥi of Lunel, whom we cited in this chapter, was born and raised in that Provençal city. However he led an itinerant life. During the years 1204-1205 he was in Toledo where he composed his work *Sepher Hamanhig* in which he describes the customs of the cities through which he passed. Among those scholars whom he quotes are a rabbi of Narbonne and Rashi.[108] Gross is of the opinion that Hayarḥi may actually have copied part of the *Mahzor Vitry*, a work of Simḥah ben Shemuel of Vitry, a student of Rashi.[109] The following citation from *Sepher Hamanhig* illustrates the numerous places that Hayarḥi had either personally visited or was familiar with:

ולא ראיתי בצרפת ובפרובנצא ולא באלמניה וקלפניא ובורגניא וכל ארץ איי
הים ולא שמעתי שמריחין אך במקומות מועטים בספרד שמעתי שמריחין.[110]

And I did not see [the inhaling of aromatic spices on a Saturday night which is a festival] either in France and Provence, or in Germany, Champagne, Burgundy, and all of the Land of the Island of the Sea (Britain). And I did not hear that they inhale [them]; but in a few places in Spain I heard that they inhale [them].

---

[105] Gross, *Gallia Judaica*, p. 411.
[106] W. Bacher, "Abraham ibn Ezra dans le nord de la France," *REJ*, XVII (1896), 300-304.
[107] Gross, *Gallia Judaica*, p. 231.
[108] *Sepher Hamanhig:* "Hilkhot Pesaḥ," p. 126, paragraph 40.
[109] Gross, *Gallia Judaica*, p. 283.
[110] *Sepher Hamanhig*, p. 131, paragraph 63.

Spain-Narbonne

(1) Rabbi Benjamin of Tudela left Saragossa, Spain in 1160, and in thirteen years visited nearly three hundred places in Provence, Italy, Greece, Cilicia, Palestine, Mesopotamia, Persia and India; returning by way of Egypt and Sicily.[111] He naturally visited Narbonne.[112] His visit took place in 1167, when Avraham ben Yitzhak was president of its rabbinical college.[113] This Spanish traveler called Narbonne a "city pre-eminent for learning; thence the Torah (Law) goes forth to all countries. Sages and illustrious men abide here."[114]

(2) Avraham ibn David of Toledo in his *Sepher Hakabbalah* compared the talmudic academy of Narbonne to those of Babylon, and he praised its scholars.[115]

(3) Yoseph ben Yitzhak Kimhi (1110-1175), the famous grammarian, biblical commentator, philosopher and *homme de lettres*, who originated in Spain, established himself in Narbonne, as did his equally illustrious sons Moses (1150-1200) and David (1160-1232).[116]

Narbonne-Northern France

Channels of communication between Narbonne and Northern France were likewise open to traveling scholars. We have already observed the cases of Avraham ibn Ezra and Hayarhi.

(1) Yoseph Tov Elem ("Bonfils") ben Shemuel, who lived in the middle of the eleventh century, originated in Narbonne but moved to Limoges and Anjou. This scholar composed a ritual prayer book, and is referred to by Rabbeinu Tam (*Sepher Hayashar*, 74a) and by Simhah ben Shemuel of Vitry (*Mahzor Vitry*, n⁰ˢ 262 and 284).[117]

---

[111] Armand Kaminka, "Benjamin of Tudela," *The Universal Jewish Encyclopedia*; Marcus Nathan Adler, tr. and ed., *The Itinerary of Benjamin of Tudela. Critical Text, Translation and Commentary* (London, 1907).
[112] *The Itinerary*, I, 2, p. 2.
[113] Gross, *Gallia Judaica*, p. 417.
[114] *The Itinerary*, I, 2, p. 2. Cf. Gross, *Gallia Judaica*, p. 406.
[115] Gross, *Gallia Judaica*, p. 406.
[116] Gross, *Gallia Judaica*, p. 417.
[117] *Ibid.*, p. 308.

(2) References to the Scholars of Narbonne are to be found in many Northern sources — e.g., the Tosafists (post-Rashi exegetes) on *Tractate Sabbath,* 26b; and *Baba Batra,* 97b; Rabbeinu Tam (*Sepher Hayashar,* 64); and the *Mahzor Vitry* refer to customs of that city. [118]

Contacts Between France and the Land of Israel

Parallel to the intercourse between Spain and Northern France, there existed a continuous flow of Jewish travelers between Western Europe and the Holy Land, and there was a constant flow of scholarly information between these two portions of the globe. [119]

Responsa

When it was impossible for scholars to journey in order to obtain information, such knowledge was often gained through epistles:

> The Responsa addressed by rabbinical authorities to individuals or to communities who had submitted difficult questions to them for solution constitute a special genus of post-Biblical literature. Lively relations were established among the Jews of the most widely separated countries; an active correspondence went on between scholars of Babylon, Northern Africa, Spain, France, Germany and Italy. [120]

Rashi engaged in a most extensive correspondence. [121]

Itinerant Preachers

Perhaps one of the most important means by which large masses of Jews in Northern France could learn about the practices of their brethren in the south was through the institution of traveling preachers. Menahem Glenn describes them in the following manner:

> In addition to the scholars, travelling preachers were visiting Jewish settlements and communities and delivering their

---

[118] *Mahzor Vitry,* nos. 141, 339, 348 et passim. See also Gross, *op. cit.,* p. 406.
[119] Glenn, "On Rashi's Life and Teachings," *Rashi,* ed. S. Federbush, pp. 138-139.
[120] Liber, *Rashi,* p. 162.
[121] I. K. Mikliszanski, "*Hayyei Hamoreh,*" *Rashi: His Teachings and Personality,* ed. Federbush, p. 13.

homilies on the Sabbath before the local congregations. Thus there developed a school of darshanim, homiletical preachers like Moses Hadarshan of Narbonne whom Rashi quotes quite often.[122]

Levi the brother of Mosheh Hadarshan settled in Montolieu (southern France).[123] Rabbeinu Tam mentions him in his elegy.[124]

Migrations

One final way in which Jews of northern France could have either directly or indirectly come into contact with the customs of Spain would be through migrations. In 1140 a large number of Jews migrated from Narbonne to Anjou, Poitou, and other French provinces.[125] We have already seen in our discussion of the synods that channels of communication existed between Anjou, Poitou and Troyes.

The above facts, in my opinion, demonstrate that ample opportunity existed for the Jews of Troyes to have come into contact with their Sephardic coreligionists. As the Passover *Seder* is perhaps the most widely-practiced religious ritual, it likewise appears to me highly probable that exchange of opinion on this matter did take place (as evidenced e.g., by descriptions of this ritual by Hayarḥi). Chrétien could thus have learned of this rite either directly or indirectly through contact with Sephardic Jews.

---

[122] Glenn, "On Rashi's Life and Teachings," *Rashi*, ed. Federbush, p. 138. Rashi cites Moses Hadarshan (commentary on Numbers 7:18 and 15:4) under the name *Yisod*. Naḥmanides (Rabbi Mosheh ben Naḥman, the "Ramban," Spanish talmudist, kabbalist, and biblical exegete, 1194-1270) in his biblical commentaries (Genesis 35:8, Numbers 19:3, 26:48 and 32:42) refers to him under the appelation *Midrash* (Gross, *Gallia Judaica*, pp. 405, 411).

[123] Gross, *Gallia Judaica*, p. 411; *Sepher Hayashar*, 64b.

[124] Gross, *Gallia Judaica*, ibid. and p. 320.

[125] Gross, *Gallia Judaica*, p. 320.

CHAPTER IV

THE DEVELOPMENT OF PERCEVAL

In the preceding chapter we have attempted to demonstrate that the Judaic theory accounts for a greater number of details found in Chrétien's narrative than do the two major Grail theories. We have, however, purposely avoided discussing two questions of capital importance to the comprehension of the Grail episode and of the work as a whole: how would Perceval's unasked questions have effected the re-establishment of the Fisher King's realm, and why did Chrétien choose to place a representation of the Jewish *Seder* in the heart of his romance? Since, as we shall see, the answers to both of these questions are dependent upon a knowledge of the main protagonist's psychological and professional evolution we must devote this chapter to tracing the development of our hero so that we may determine the importance of the Grail episode to the structure of the romance and to the evolution of its main character.[1]

---

[1] I formulated my analysis and interpretation of *Le Conte du Graal* without the aid of secondary source material. However, after I completed my interpretation, I consulted such studies as Jean Frappier, *Chrétien de Troyes* and *Perceval* (cited above); Wilhelm Kellermann, *Aufbaustil und Weltbild Chrestien von Troyes im Percevalroman* (Tübingen, 1967); Reto Bezzola, *Le Sens de l'aventure et de l'amour (Chrétien de Troyes)* (Paris, 1947) and *Les Origines et la formation de la littérature courtoise en Occident* (Paris, 1963); David C. Fowler, *Prowess and Charity in the Perceval of Chrétien de Troyes* (Seattle, 1959); Erich Köhler, "Les Romans de Chrétien de Troyes," *Revue de l'Institut de Sociologie*, XXXVI (1963), 271-284 (N.B. This article is a condensation of Köhler's book *Ideal und Wirklichkeit in der höfischen Epik — Studien zur Form der Frühen Artus-und-Graldichtung. Beihefte zur Z.R.P.;* Heft 97. [Tübingen, 1956] which was unavailable to me); and Peter Haidu, *Aesthetic Distance in Chrétien de Troyes: Irony and Comedy in*

PLATE 9. Passover Plate. Pewter. Baruch Schechter of Fuerth, 1773.

PLATE 10. *Seder* Plate. Silver. Germany, 19th Century.

Le Conte du Graal describes the courtly, intellectual and moral development of a young man. It is in many ways an exodus story of the psyche and as such presents structural parallels with that of the biblical Exodus. It is the story of a youth's journey from a benign but innocent isolation, through the arduous desert of worldly involvement, to an eventual arrival upon a new summit of Christianity and humanity. It is in part the story of how young Perceval becomes a highly esteemed knight but more important, it is the story of how this youth comes to learn about the Passion and to receive Holy Communion.[2] To attain this level of spiritual development, he must acquire

---

Cligès and Perceval (Geneva, 1968). In many instances, these studies confirmed my own interpretations while in other cases they differed from my readings. I shall refer to these sources when an idea I am advancing requires further elucidation. For a detailed analysis of the structure of the romance, including schematic representations of Perceval's professional and moral developments see my thesis, "Chrétien's Grail: A Jewish Rite? A New Investigation Based Upon Medieval Hebraic Sources," Cornell University, 1970, pp. 109-145. Cf. Eugène J. Weinraub, "Chrétien's Grail: A Jewish Rite? A New Investigation Based Upon Medieval Hebraic Sources" (Daniel Potier) *Cahiers de Civilisation Médiévale* XIV (1971), 399-401 and Eugene J. Weinraub, "Chrétien's Grail: A Jewish Rite? A New Investigation Based Upon Medieval Hebraic Sources," *Dissertation Abstracts International,* XXXI (1971) 4738A.

[2] Fowler, Kellerman and Bezzola examine the juxtaposition between Perceval's courtly or professional development and his religious or moral evolution. Kellermann (*Aufbaustil,* pp. 7-23, 84-122, 205-220) sees a parallel between the structure and style of this romance. The *enjambement des scènes* and the binary (ABAB) schema of this work is a result of its dual orientation toward the spiritual and toward the courtly. In the *Perceval* the spiritual element enhances the secular but does not eclipse it: Perceval, at the conclusion of the hermitage episode will be a Chrisitian knight. Gauvain will conquer the lance (worldly success). Perceval will conquer the grail (non-liturgical spiritual achievement).

Bezzola (*Les Origines* I, 427) views both the grail and lance as symbols of an ideal which elevates secular knighthood to holy knighthood.

Fowler, too, views the *Perceval* as a conflict between knightly, *Prowess* and Christian *Charity*. This schema contains subjacent Freudian undertones of a mother-father conflict. In the Good Friday episode *Charity* triumphs over *Prowess* and the mother-father conflict is resolved in the all embracing love of God (*Prowess and Charity,* especially pp. 57-60).

Gabriel John Brogyanyi ("Will and Motivation in the Romances of Chrétien de Troyes," Thesis, Cornell University, 1969, pp. 67-72; 97-99) sees a "plateau" structure in Chrétien's works. The hero mounts to a certain level of achievement, falls and eventually rehabilitates himself, arriving on a plateau of regained mastery. In the *Perceval* Brogyanyi correctly distinguished a dichotomy between the hero's chivalric development, which steadily

two distinct but interrelated abilities: the ability to ask proper questions and the capacity to comprehend their answers. But to acquire these, Perceval must first learn to think for himself, take responsibility for his own decisions, lose his egotism and show consideration for others. He must commit, recognize, atone for and correct his errors (sins), experience personal anguish and find the strength to cry.

Let us now examine more thoroughly the evolution of this intriguing character.[3] In the opening scenes (Perceval in the forest and his subsequent encounters with the knights, his mother, the Tent Maiden and King Arthur [69-1066]) we may observe that our hero possesses many admirable qualities which foretell his future success in knightly endeavors. He is of noble birth (as witnessed by the facts that his mother owns a manor and employs harrowers [81-82], that he is referred to as *seignor* [311], that he is comely [977], that he can appreciate nature [85-90],[4] and that he has a natural compulsion to become a knight [316-319]). He possesses a quick, intelligent mind (as his interrogations of the knights and his mother demonstrate [172-

---

advances, and his moral sensitivity which rises and falls. However, I question Brogyanyi's assertion that Perceval's moment of achievement is at the Castle of Beaurepaire and that, after his fall, he does not regain his former level of moral development due to the incompletion of the romance.

[3] Haidu (*Aesthetic Distance*, passim) interprets the *Perceval* as being essentially ironic in nature. He questions the entire notion of Perceval's development. According to him, Perceval remains a simpleton even at the conclusion of the Good Friday episode (*Ibid.*, p. 224). In this chapter I should like to demonstrate that a moral and professional development does take place. See David Fowler (*Prowess and Charity*, passim) and especially Wilhelm Kellermann (*Aufbaustil*, pp. 16-18, 194-202) for a discussion of Perceval's development.

[4] Frappier, *Perceval*, p. 37:

> Déjà l'origine aristocratique de l'enfant se manifeste dans le plaisir que lui cause le chant des oiseaux dans la forêt.... Conception médiévale exprimée plus d'une fois par les poètes et les romanciers courtois: selon eux, le ramage des oiseaux chanteurs était dépourvu de sens pour les vilains, mais dans l'âme des chevaliers ils éveillaient des résonances particulières, évoquaient en eux l'amour, les tournois les exploits accomplis....

Cf. Lucien Foulet, *Glossary of the First Continuation*, Vol. III, pt. 2 *The Continuations of the Old French Perceval of Chretien de Troyes*, ed. William Roach (Philadelphia, 1955), p. 203:

> *oisel* s.m. fr.... Mais les oiseaux ne sont pas toujours considérés comme un mets de choix: par leurs chants ils charment l'oreille et le cœur de ceux qui les écoutent. On mentionne volontiers dans nos romans ce pouvoir qu'ils ont.

342; 383-402]), and he is highly conscious of the value of language. Thus the clairvoyant members of King Arthur's court easily discern the youth's inherent nobility, and both the omniscient Arthur and the Maiden Who Laughed predict his future professional success (1039-1944, 1282-1300).

However, there are many negative features about this adolescent. He is naive, clumsy, unpolished in speech and action, and unskilled in the use of arms other than his javelin. He is, therefore, on the symbolic level most fittingly accoutred in coarse Welsh clothing — clothing which he will not shed until he will arrive upon a higher plane of chivalric behavior. But, more significant, Perceval is incapable of thinking for himself. When presented with a new situation he mechanically falls back upon the simplistic maxims of his mother (114-116, 142-144, 658, 682-683; cf. 1363, 1402, 1674). If at the opening of the romance it may be assumed that Perceval has done no evil, it is because he has not yet been faced with the opportunity of doing so. But though his mother's oversimplified teachings may suffice for determining the difference between devils and angels, in cases where such a clearly discernable polarity does not exist, Perceval would be incapable of arriving at correct moral judgments. He blindly substitutes his mother's three lessons in chivalry (help ladies, keep company with noble men, worship in a church [527-594]) which he does not comprehend (as witnessed by his confusion of a lover's tent with a church [655] and his behavior with the Tent Maiden [552-763]) for her misunderstood and mechanically followed naive, religious teachings.[6] As he is incapable of individual thought, he does not possess an identity and is thus symbolically ignorant of his name, which for Chrétien revealed one's character ("Par le sornom connoist on l'ome." [562]).[7] All that Perceval knows of himself or that Chrétien's audience knows of him, is that he is the "widow's son" (74).

---

[5] Perceval's carefully constructed interrogation of his mother (383-402) demonstrates this.

[6] For an authoritative discussion of Perceval's theocentric religion see Imbs, "L'Elément religieux," *Les Romans du Graal*, pp. 31-53. Haidu (*Aesthetic Distance*, pp. 129-130) explains that because Perceval is isolated from society, he cannot comprehend religion which is a function of society and which exists in the context of a society.

[7] Bezzola was the first to call attention to the importance of the *name* in *Perceval* as in all medieval literature. He recalls the significance of the *senhal* to the Troubadours and states in reference to Perceval:

In the opening episodes Perceval repeatedly demonstrates a high degree of egocentricity. He is extremely impatient (491-494, 972-973, 986-990, 1090-1092) and shows neither consideration for, nor awareness of, others. He does not react emotionally either to his mother's first fainting, or to her persistent crying and cajoling, or to her fainting upon his departure. Fully aware that his mother may have just perished, Perceval, with an indifference not unlike that of Camus's Stranger, having crossed the moat separating himself from the outside world, rides off with perfect *sang froid* into the dark forest (620-630). [8]

> Par son nom, Perceval le Gallois, il entrevoit pour la première fois le fond de sa personnalité. Jusque-là, il n'avait qu'une existence relative: il était, par rapport aux autres, "beau fils," "beau frère," "beau sire." Désormais il a une existence propre, bien qu'elle soit encore pour lui problématique.... Tout nom comporte une mission.... Le sens mystique du nom se révèle par la réaction subite de la demoiselle. (*Le Sens de l'aventure*, p. 56)

Frappier (*Perceval*, p. 61) likewise notes that in medieval symbolism there is a relationship between one's name and one's personality: "Le nom est comme une consécration de la personnalité.... L'intuition de son nom coincide chez Perceval avec l'intuition de sa véritable personnalité." Haidu (*Aesthetic Distance*, pp. 177-179), however, believes that Chrétien deliberately introduced an absurd element into his story when he included the episodes dealing with Perceval's name.

[8] The exact nature of Perceval's sin has been the subject of much discussion. Marx (*La Légende arthurienne et le Graal*, p. 207n.) claims that the explanation of Perceval's failure to have asked the proper questions due to his having abandoned his mother, is "une absurdité ajoutée à l'histoire." Similarly, Frappier (*Perceval*, p. 60n.) believes that this explanation was not a part of the original story. However, he denies that it is absurd. For him, Perceval's sin was not his having left his mother, since he had permission to do so, but rather, his failure to turn back when he saw her fallen upon the ground. Fowler (*Prowess and Charity*, p. 56) believes Perceval's sin was "the abandonment of what his mother told him, that is, the spiritual ideal, the love of God." I disagree with both Fowler and Marx on this issue. Since Perceval never fully understood the ideal of the "love of God" he could not have abandoned it. As I shall attempt to demonstrate that the only way for Perceval to arrive at such an understanding is by leaving his mother's manor, I do not believe that this act constituted his sin.

Inasmuch as both the Hermit (6394) and Perceval's cousin (3594) describe the youth's sin as being the grief or pain (*doel*) he had inflicted upon his mother, I am of the opinion that Perceval's *pechiez* resided in his egotism which is manifested in the callous *manner* by which he abandoned her; his failure to have attempted to lessen her fears.

When she had fallen to the ground, it may have already been too late for Perceval to have been able to rectify the situation. It is this egocentricity

Perceval pays no attention to his mother's accounts of his lineage and of the Passion (the comprehension of which presupposes an ability to empathize with the plight of others). He is oblivious of the Tent Maiden's distress (734-763), and no doubt, due to his overexaggerated self-preoccupation while in her presence he is unable to even recognize this unfortunate girl on a future occasion (3785-3790), just as he is later incapable of recognizing his cousin *with whom he had been raised* (3596-3599). He cares nothing for the Red Knight's grievances (865-897) nor for the distress of King Arthur, Guinevere, the Maiden who Laughed, and the court fool (859-860, 898-899, 1063-1066). He is interested only in his own primary needs: his stomach (491-499) — which constitutes the object of his prayers (664-665) — and his immediate goal of becoming a knight (333-336, 493-494).

Indeed as foretold by the very first scenes, where he preferred to strike what he believed to be devils rather than ward them off by the sign of the cross (121), and where he twice declared knights to be more beautiful than angels (179, 393-394), Perceval will now substitute a new religion of arms for his former puerile religious beliefs. But as Perceval has confused the procurement of arms with becoming a knight ("Chevalier m'a fait / Li rois qui bone aventure ait" [1369-1370]), he is incapable of perceiving anything deeper in knighthood than external appearance. He will thus be interested only in obtaining the armor of the slain knight and will insist upon retaining his coarse Welsh clothing beneath his arms (1161-1165).

Perceval's victory over the Red Knight, however, marks the beginning of his professional and moral evolution. No sooner does Perceval don the fallen knight's armor than the crude youth becomes cognizant of other human beings. He now pledges to avenge the shame of the Maiden Who Laughed and requests Yvonet to return King Arthur's cup, which the Red Knight had stolen, to its rightful owner (1197-1206). Chrétien underlines this metamorphosis and hints at the youth's future chivalric development by remarking that the fallen knight's helmet becomes the youth well (1182).

As Perceval evolves in knightly prowess and *courtoisie* through his subsequent associations with Gornemant de Goort, who teaches

---

which will prevent Perceval from asking the proper questions at the Grail Castle.

him the fundamentals of knighthood (1305-1609) and Blancheflor for whom he defeats two valiant knights (1609-2975), his attitude towards people simultaneously improves.[9] Twice, during the course of these episodes, he recalls the Maiden Who Laughed (2313-2323, 2692-2699), and gradually, with ever increasing frequency, he remembers his mother whom he had abandoned (1580-1591, 1699-1702, 2914-2921, 2960-2971, 2980-2984) and even gives up his immediate economic happiness, to seek her out. On the symbolic level, as Perceval acquires new chivalric and moral dimension, he is addressed with progressively more respectful terms of salutation. Thus Gornemant, after initially addressing the naive lad with the condescending form *biax frere* (1364), later addresses his newly dubbed protégé with the egalitarian forms *amis* and *biax amis* (1607, 1616). Blancheflor, in turn, then greets her young chevalier with the deferential forms *sire* and *biax sire* (1732, 1835, 1883, 2146).[10] Similarly, after Perceval acquires a deeper practical knowledge and training in the physical skills required of knighthood, this youth symbolically receives from Gornemant more comely undergarments to replace his crude Welsh clothing (1600-1615).

However, despite Perceval's martial, courtly, and moral advancement, he has far to go achieve full self-realization. He is unaware that *chevalerie* entails more than arms handling, and, incapable of critical thought, he merely substitutes Gornemant's advice, which he does not fully comprehend, for that of his mother. Thus, having misinterpreted Gornemant's caveat against speaking *too much* as an order not to speak at all, Perceval feels obliged to blindly apply this maxim without regard for the occasion, and he would have sat mutely beside Blancheflor for an indefinite period of time had the damsel not taken the initiative and addressed a question to him (1877-1883). He is impatient (1720-21, 1736-1738) and is still preoccupied with his *amour propre*. He revels in his newly acquired title *chevalier* (1728), and he engaged (and subsequently spared) the two knights Anguingueron and Clamadeu, in part, because of his vanity and desire for

---

[9] Bezzola (*Le Sens de l'aventure*, p. 57) briefly speaks of Perceval's lack of consideration for others in relation to Perceval's encounter with his cousin. Unfortunately, he does not develop this theme.

[10] For a discussion of these forms see William Averill Stowell, *Old-French Titles of Respect in Direct Address* (Baltimore, 1908), pp. 19, 37-38; 142-143, 191-197, 212-215.

self-assertion (2118-2124, 2254-2258). Though Perceval is concerned with learning about his mother's welfare, there is some doubt about the extent of his emotional preoccupation with her, since the prospect of her death does not elicit quite so great an emotional response on his part as one would perhaps expect (2964-2965, 2968-2971). But more important, Perceval still does not believe that he has committed a sin against his mother; and, though he feels that he is acting in her best interest, he imagines, in his egocentricity, that he can dispose of her destiny as freely as he chooses (2960-2963).

In the Grail episode, Perceval will climb to a slightly higher moral plane. He will not, however, rid himself totally of his immaturity and egocentricity.

As Perceval wanders on his journey, recalling his mother, and praying for her well-being (2980-2984), he arrives at a river. He exclaims that, were he able to cross the stream, he would be able to find her (2990-2993). Such an action under the proper conditions would be a short-cut to the conclusion of the romance; for were his mother indeed alive, he would perhaps be able to learn about the Fisher King and the grail directly from her; while if she were dead, he would perhaps become aware of having sinned and thus, with repentance, be able at a later date to ask the appropriate questions of the Fisher King. However, Perceval is not morally ready, i.e., his personal sensitivity is not sufficiently developed, for him to reap such a reward. He is therefore unable to cross this stream which the Fisher King can traverse with ease. Chrétien perhaps hints at the young knight's need for further moral development by having the Fisher King reply to Perceval's request for shelter (physical well-being): "You will have need of that *and more*, I believe" (3026-3027).

But if in the presence of the Fisher King Perceval shows some concern for his mother; if he is capable of speaking in a decorous manner (3110-3111); and if he is even honored by being allowed to sit next to his host, by being addressed with the egalitarian epithet *amis* (3107-3331), and by being given a beautiful sword destined for one who could use it well (3151-3153, 3167-3168), Perceval still retains many of his former traits. He is impatient, and he still cannot fully relate to other human beings. He is exceedingly quick to curse the Fisherman, when, due to his own lack of perception, he cannot distinguish the Fisher King's castle (3042-3043). Chrétien ridicules this lack of maturity by forcing Perceval to swallow his words:

> Si se loe del pescheor;
> Ne l'apele mais traïtor
> Ne desloial ne mençoignier,
> Des que il trove ou hebergier. (3061-3064)

Though the Fisher King, is aware of the limitations of arms and recognizes that the sword with the fancy hangings is not infallible (3136-3143), Perceval, who has not advanced in this respect beyond the opening scenes of the romance, still believes that the sword alone will be enough to sustain him (3178-3179). Perceval is still lacking in identity, i.e., he is still nameless. He knows nothing of his own lineage nor who his host is, nor does he seem interested enough to inquire. Because he is all too conscious of his own importance and of the impression he wished to project upon others ("Et crient, se il le demandast, / Qu'en le tenist a vilonie" [3210-3211]), he is morally incapable of asking his host the appropriate questions about the grail, that would lead to the re-establishment of the Fisher King's reign and to a sort of Kingdom of God on earth. He would furthermore, at this point, be incapable of understanding the answers to his unasked questions since their comprehension implies an awareness of the existence of others, — i.e. his lineage (the Fisher King and the ascetic) and Jesus — and an ability to empathize with their plight — an ability which this egocentric youth does not yet possess. Were he already at the level where he could recognize his sins and bear their weight, i.e., know that he is not a paragon of virtue, he would have had a sufficient lack of self-consciousness to overcome his restraints and ask what he honestly desired to know. Instead he blindly follows Gornemant's advice, which he misinterpreted, hoping that it will provide him with a shortcut to correct behavior in all situations and thus relieve him of the responsibility of thinking for himself.

The Grail episode, however, represents a turning point in the romance. Till this point, Perceval had been committing errors. From now on, he will begin to rectify them. Though he will soon achieve complete professional development, the completion of his moral education will require a longer period of time.

In the presence of his cousin, Perceval will rise on the scale of moral value to the extent where he will gain a slight awareness of the fact that he had done wrong in regard to his behavior with the Fisher King. With this improved knowledge of his relative capacities, he will gain some insight into his own identity, and will thus be privileged, on the symbolic, level, to correctly divine his name (3573-3577), and to learn from his cousin more about himself and about her relationship to him. But though Perceval is now capable of appreciating the moral worth of a person rather than his material value:

— "Pucele, par le Salveor,
Ne sai s'il est peschiere ou rois,
Mais molt est sages et cortois," (3496-3498)

and though Perceval recognizes that his sword may not be as infallible as he had once thought:

— "Certes, or me seroit molt grief,
Fait Perchevax, se ele fraint," (3686-3687)

he is still totally unaware of having sinned against his mother, and other than admitting that his cousin brought him bad tidings, he exhibits little emotional response to the news of his mother's death (" 'Autre voie m'estuet tenir" [3625]; "Les mors as mors, les vis as vis" [3630]) and to the tragic story of the Fisher King.

After this meeting, Perceval will progress morally to the extent where he will become fully aware of having committed an error and be able to make amends for it. Though when Perceval approaches the Tent Maiden, he neither recognizes her nor recalls that he had at one time wronged her, he now has sufficient personal sensitivity to empathize with her plight (3796-3804), and when he comes to learn that he was the cause of this maiden's suffering, he readily admits his guilt (3901-3910). After defeating the Proud Knight, whose skill Gauvain later describes in superlative terms (4091-4095), Perceval demonstrates his growing concern for others by requiring his adversary to forgive his lady (the Tent Maiden) for his ill-founded suspicions before he obtains his own pardon (3938-3939). Perceval places the welfare of this unfortunate girl above his own honor by requiring the defeated Proud Knight to see to it that his mistress' wounds are fully healed before setting forth as his prisoner for King Arthur's court (3950-3956). On previous occasions, when Perceval had defeated a knight, he had required his antagonist to report to the Maiden Who Laughed that the would avenge her. Now, however, when forcing the Proud Knight to perform this task, Perceval, for the first time, considers the resulting amelioration in the maiden's psychological condition (3975-3980).

Perceval now rises to such a high degree of moral value that he is capable of meditating upon the qualities of his mistress (4450-4456). He will, after avenging the honor of the Maiden Who Laughed (4307-4316), be privileged to meet the courtly knight Gauvain (by whom he is addressed as *biax sire* [4486]) and arrive with him as equals at King Arthur's court (4501, 4545), where Perceval's courteous behavior will make amends for his former indifference (4587). Perceval now seems surer of his identity, giving Gauvain his name without any hesitation (4482-4483).

Though Perceval is, however, at the peak of his knightly career, this is not enough for Chrétien. If he is still not aware that there are institutions and values which surpass *chevalerie*; if he is still unaware that it is naive to believe one can indescriminately apply a series of elaborately constructed rules of conduct with equal validity to all situations; if he is still not completely cognizant of God's presence, unconscious of having sinned against his fellow man, unable to forget his own importance, and unable to express his inner emotions, then all of his valor and professional status is meaningless.

It is precisely these lessons which Perceval has yet to learn. Thus the Loathly Damsel arrives at King Arthur's court to help bring the youth to this realization. After rebuking Perceval for not having been outspoken enough to ask the Fisher King the appropriate questions at the appropriate time; after depicting in almost eschatological terms the pacific and harmonious reign of the Fisher King which Perceval could have re-established by his questions; and after describing the tragedy which is now destined to befall the Fisher King and his people; she tells of knightly adventures, whose successful completion would bring unprecedented honor upon those who undertake them (4685-4714).

But Perceval, presumably affected by her words, voluntarily gives up the vainglorious pursuits to which the best of Arthur's knights pledge themselves and dedicates himself to seeking the answers to the questions he had failed to ask, perhaps hoping thereby to avert the tragedy (4727-4740).

Though Perceval's goal is meritorious, his means of achieving it — physical hardship and prowess — are inappropriate. Perceval's shortcomings at the Fisher King's castle contained deeper moral undertones. As Perceval was morally incapable of asking the questions at the Grail Castle because his pride prevented him from recognizing that he had sinned, he will continue to remain incapable of gaining this information until he becomes cognizant of his transgression and remedies it by the only means possible — sincere repentance. In order to achieve this awareness, however, Perceval must first experience personal anguish. Thus our hero now suffers a lapse so that he may later emerge upon a higher spiritual plane.

Perceval's attempt at re-establishing the Fisher King's realm by physical means results in utter failure. Not only does he fail to make amends for his error (6378), but he totally forgets God. Though for five years he has done chivalrous deeds and sent sixty famous knights to King Arthur's court as prisoners (6224-6235), all these heroic acts have amounted to evil (6364-6367). We thus find our hero aimlessly wandering in a spiritual as well as physical desert ("Au chief des cinc ans si avint / Que il par un desert aloit" [6238-6239]).

The deep personal anguish which Perceval had suffered during this period had undoubtedly left its mark upon him. Thus, when he dramatically encounters the penitent pilgrims, learns from them that it is Good Friday, and hears from their lips the story of the Passion (6266-6300), he suddenly experiences for the first time a strong sense of sin. For the first time in the romance he breaks down in tears and is truly penitent (6315-6317, 6333-6337).

Seeking the hermit, Perceval now possesses both spiritual *and* physical direction. In the presence of this saintly man, the youth forgets his own importance (for the first time Chrétien describes him as humble) and bows to the spiritual superiority of the hermit. By gestures and by tears Perceval demonstrates his contrition (6348-6359).

Perceval confesses those sins of which he is aware, namely, that he had forgotten God and had done evil. These he attributes to his silence in the Fisher King's castle. The hermit however, upon learning his visitor's name, informs him of a sin of which Perceval had been totally unaware, the fact that he had caused his mother's death by having abandoned her:

> "Uns pechiez dont tu ne sez mot:
> Ce fu li doels que ta mere ot
> De toi quant departis de li,
> Que pasmee a terre chaï
> Al chief del pont devant la porte,

> Et de cel doel fu ele morte.
> Por le pechié que tu en as
> T'avient que rien n'en demandas
> De la lance ne del graal,
> Si t'en sont avenu maint mal;" (6393-6402)

It was this sin that had rendered Perceval morally incapable of asking the Fisher King the questions,[11] "Pechie[z] la langue te trencha," says the hermit (6409). Now that Perceval through his humility is able to recognize his transgression, he is worthy of learning the mystery of the Grail Castle:

> "Cil qui l'en en sert est mes frere,
> Ma suer et soe fu ta mere;
> Et del riche Pescheor croi
> Qu'il est fix a icelui roi
> Qu'en cel gr[a]al servir se fait." (6415-6419)

In learning the answers to the question "Who is served with the grail," i.e., learning about or appreciating *others,* Perceval is actually learning about his *own* history, or lineage, i.e., his own identity. The hermit now entreats Perceval to be truly repentant (6441) and gives him essentially the same advice his mother had offered him at the beginning of the romance: worship in a church, honor good men, and help maidens (6439-6470). Perceval now delights in the mass, worships the cross (6493-6496) and receives communion (6512-6513).

Because the hermit describes Perceval as having returned to a position he had formerly occupied:

> "Ce weil que por tes pechiez faces,
> Se ravoir veus totes tes graces
> Issi com tu avoir les seus," (6471-6473)

and because so much of the last episode reminds us of the beginning of the romance, we may rightly ask ourselves. Was Perceval's journey at all necessary? Could Perceval have achieved the same ends by

---

[11] Frappier (*Perceval,* p. 79) interprets v. 6393 ("Uns pechiez don tu ne sez mot," as being inexact, since Perceval's cousin had already informed him of his sins (vv. 3593-3595). I prefer to interpret v. 6393 literally. Though Perceval had been *told* of his sin, by his cousin, he was, due to egocentricity, incapable of fully comprehending her words, just as in the opening scene he had been incapable of understanding his mother's lessons.

staying at home with his mother? Did his mother not tell him of the Passion? Did she not begin to explain to him about his lineage, e.g., his father who was wounded in the identical manner as the Fisher King? Might she not have eventually told him of his cousin, the Fisher King, and of his uncle, the ascetic? Could Perceval not have effected his own salvation as well as that of the Fisher King by remaining isolated in his mother's manor?

Though Chrétien does not answer such questions directly, we may hypothesize on the basis of what he has said in the romance that his answer would have been negative. Perceval's journey was not a cyclic one (a return to a starting point) but rather a helical one (a return in the direction of one's starting point but to a higher plane). Though from a factual point of view Perceval could have learned all he needed to know from his mother, without *his own* practical experience, such lessons would have been meaningless: "Li vallés entent molt petit / A che que sa mere li dist" (489-490). It is only through committing *his own* sins and suffering because of them that Perceval can appreciate the significance of the Passion — of one individual taking upon himself the sins of *all mankind* and suffering for them. Though he had heard the story of the Passion from his mother, and had recited a credo which presumably contained an allusion to it, he previously had experienced neither feeling nor personal involvement with this event and thus had missed its true significance. It is only after feeling the weight of his own sins that Perceval can worship the cross and *weep* over his sins: ("Aprés le service aoura / La crois et ses pechiez plora." [6495-6496]). It is only now, after finally being able to understand others, and himself, that he can comprehend the significance of the Passion and be worthy of receiving the body of Jesus within himself:

> Issi Perchevax *reconnut*
> Que Diex el vendredi rechut
> Mort et si fu crucefiiez
> A le Pasque communiiez
> Fu Perchevax mult dignement. (6509-6513) [12]

---

[12] Italics, my own.

CHAPTER V

INTERPRETATION AND CONCLUSIONS

After having traced Perceval's moral and spiritual evolution, we are now able to answer our two problems: how Perceval's unasked questions could have brought about the Fisher King's redemption, and why Chrétien should have chosen to place a representation of a *Seder* in the heart of his work.

Before proceeding, let us make some general observations on Chrétien's story:

1. The questions Perceval was supposed to have asked would have led to a knowledge of his own history or lineage through recognition of the identity of the ascetic.

2. The asking of these questions would have resulted in the re-establishment of the Fisher King's reign, with beneficent results accruing to his subjects and to Perceval (3590).

3. Because Perceval was incapable of asking these questions, these benefic results did not occur.

If we now re-examine the events of Chrétien's narrative in the context of the *Seder*, we find that they acquire added significance. We may recall that in the *Seder* the questions, which the youngest child is supposed to ask, result in the recounting of the Exodus story by the officiant.[1] However, according to the liturgy of the Passover *Seder*, this abstract act of narration is transformed into concrete reality. Thus, on a spiritual level all the participants in the ceremony

---

[1] The traditional answer begins: "*Avadim Hayinu....*" ("We were slaves unto Pharaoh in Egypt.")

PLATE 11. *Seder* Night. Painting. Moritz Oppenheim (1799-1822).

PLATE 12. *Above:* Agents of the Inquisition invade a Marrano *Seder*.

Below: The Head-table of a Model *Seder* in the Israel Defense Forces. The author is seated at the right of the speaker, Brig. Gen. Gad Navon, Deputy Chief Rabbi of the Israel Defense Forces.

are changed into participants in the very Exodus as a mishnaic passage in the *Haggadah* states:

בכל דור ודור חיב אדם לראות את עצמו כאלו הוא יצא ממצרים. שנאמר
(שמות י"ג ח') והגדת לבנך ביום ההוא לאמר בעבור זה עשה ד' לי בצאתי
ממצרים: לא את אבותינו בלבד גאל הקדום ברוך הוא אלא אף אותנו גאל
עמהם. שנאמר (דברים ו' כ"ג) ואותנו הוציא משם למען הביא אותנו לתת
לנו את הארץ אשר נשבע לאבותינו: [2]

In every generation, one ought to look upon himself as if he personally had gone out of Egypt; as it is said (Exodus 13,8). "And you shall explain to your son on that day, saying "This is because of that which Yahweh did for me when I came forth out of Egypt." Not our ancestors alone did the Holy One, blessed be He redeem, but also us has He redeemed with them; as it is said (Deut. 6,23). "And he brought us out from there to lead us into the land which He swore to our fathers he would give us."

The Ḥatam Sopher, a later commentator,[3] clearly explains the meaning of this passage:

> When one understands the lesson of the Exodus from Egypt, the significance of the symbols of the *Seder* plate, then he is armed for life and it is as if he, himself, had experienced the story of Passover. Understanding the symbols is necessary for fulfilling the obligation of "explaining to one's son." In order to transmit the lesson of the liberation from bondage, one must be oneself impregnated with the meaning of slavery and its deliverance as symbolized by the Paschal sacrifice, the unleavened bread and the bitter herbs. If one understands this, it is as if he had personally left Egypt.[4]

Thus, the "Redemption" of all those present is achieved through the recounting of the Exodus story, i.e., gaining knowledge of one's history, or fundamentally, through the asking of questions, which bring about this narration.

---

[2] *Pesaḥim* X, 5 (116b); *La Haggada commentée*, p. 46.
[3] Rabbi Moses Schreiber, 1762-1830.
[4] *La Haggada commentée*, loc. cit.

On a parallel plane, we should note that a sharply defined strain of Messianic hope runs throughout the entire *Seder*. The ceremony begins and ends with a proclamation of faith and hope in the imminent return to the Land of Israel, i.e., with the coming of the Messiah.

השתא הכא לשנה הבאה בארעה דישראל.
השתא עבדי לשנה הבאה בני חורין.[5]

This year we are here, next year in the Land of Israel.
This year we are slaves, next year, free men

proclaims the Aramaic prayer *Ha Laḥma Anya*, at the opening of the *Seder*. In 13th-century France, the beginning of this prayer was recited in French to facilitate comprehension;[6] The *Seder* concludes with the statement

לשנה הבאה בירושלים.[7]

Next year in Jerusalem.

In the *Seder*, then, there are at least three different and parallel levels of meaning:

1. The Exodus story per se,
2. The symbolic transformation of the contemporary *Seder* participants into biblical children of Israel, and
3. The message of future Messianic redemption for all those present.

If we now re-examine Chrétien's Grail episode in the light of the *Seder* ritual, we arrive at the following sets of interpretations:

1. On the level of the *conte d'aventure*:

Because Perceval failed to ask the traditional questions, he did not hear the Exodus story and was thus not privileged to bring about his own and his host's symbolic "Redemption."

---

[5] *La Haggada commentée*, p. 7.
[6] *Haggadah Sheleimah*, p. 108.
[7] *La Haggada commentée*, p. 96.

2. On the moral level:

Because Perceval was not yet "impregnated with the sense of slavery and deliverance" — because he had not yet suffered personally and had not become aware of his sin, because he was too obsessed with his own importance to be aware of others, and because he was unaware of the limitations of martial prowess, he was morally incapable both of *asking* the questions, which would have occasioned the narration of the Exodus story and of *appreciating* this historical narrative (i.e., putting himself in the place of others, — the Israelites), which would have brought about his host's salvation and his own. It is precisely this humility which he must acquire during the course of the romance.

If we accept the Jewish *Seder* as a model for the Grail episode, we may infer that the Fisher King, himself, is guilty of a sin of omission and is, therefore, in part, responsible for his *rédemption manquée*. To explain, we must return to the parable of the "son who does not know how to ask" which we briefly mentioned in our third chapter. Regarding such a son, the Haggadah states:

ושאינו יודע לשאול: את פתח לו שנאמר (שמות י"ג, ח') והגדת לבנך ביום ההוא לאמור. בעבור זה עשה ד' לי בצאתי ממצרים.[8]

As for the one who does not know how to ask, you shall breach the subject to him, as it is said, "You shall explain to your son on that day saying, 'This is because of what Yahweh did for me when I came out of Egypt.'" (Exodus 13:8)

The medieval exegetes stressed the active role which the master of the house must assume in order to bring this youth to understand and to ask.[9] Though they admitted that this type of son, who is undiscerning in God's ways, His Torah, and His precepts, would not have been redeemed had he been in Egypt,[10] they recognize that it is the

---

[8] Nerson, *La Haggada commentée*, p. 20. Cf. Plate 1.

[9] Rashi (*Haggadah Commentary*, treatise *Issur Veheiter*) and the commentary of the fourteenth-century Darmstaedter Haggadah, cited by Menaḥem M. Kasher, ed. *Haggadah Sheleimah*, 3rd ed. (Jerusalem, 1967), p. 25, comment 132.

[10] See the thirteenth-century commentary of Aharon ben Yaakov Hakohen of Lunel *Orḥot Ḥayyim*, cited by Kasher (*Haggadah Sheleimah*, 3rd ed.,

officiant's duty to recount the Exodus story [11] regardless of whether or not questions are asked. [12]

Interpreting our text in light of the above, we may infer that just as Blancheflor, in the preceding episode, had taken the initiative to instigate conversation with Perceval rather than follow the established etiquette and remain silent (1877-1883), so too, in the Grail episode, it was for the Fisher King to explain to Perceval the secrets of the grail and by so doing effect his own redemption, even though at that time Perceval was incapable of redeeming himself or his host. Because the Fisher King forfeited this occasion, he must continue to suffer until a future redemption will take place.

If we quickly return to the structure of the romance, we may observe that the general outline of the Perceval tale follows that of the Exodus story. Perceval's isolation in his mother's manor, his crossing the drawbridge (623), his wandering through the large, dark forest ("le grant forest oscure" [630]) which is also described as a desert ("par un desert aloit" [6239]), his inability to ford the stream (2985-3023) and his eventual arrival at the hermitage parallel the exile of the Israelites in Egypt, their crossing the Red Sea, their wandering through the desert, Moses' inability to cross the Jordan and the eventual arrival of the children of Israel in Canaan. As far as the structure of the romance is then concerned, Chrétien, by describing the Grail episode as a *Seder* (a narration of the Exodus) would be creating a microcosm of his larger work within this important episode and perhaps thereby be providing his readers with a key to the interpretation of the work as a whole.

---

pp. 25-26, comment 136), and his contemporary, the anonymous French author of the commentary *Kol Bo* in *Haggadah shel Pesaḥ im Meah Veḥamishah-Asar Peirushim*, ed. Yisrael David Miller (Jerusalem?, 196?), p. 29.

[11] Simḥa ben Shemuel of Vitry, *Maḥzor Vitry*, ed. Shimon Halevi Horowitz (Jerusalem, 1963), p. 20. Cf. Rashi (*Commentary, Ritual Prayerbook, Issur Veheiter*); *Orḥot Ḥayyim*; Abudarham; and the *Kol Bo* in Kasher, *Haggadah Sheleimah*, 3rd ed., p. 25, comment 133.

[12] Indeed so important is the commandment to recount the Exodus story, that the thirteenth-century sage Rabbi Shimon bar Tzemaḥ ordained that even a learned man who has no son is required to ask himself the traditional questions, "since the precept of recounting the Exodus is intransigent regardless of whether or not questions were asked" (Kasher, *Haggadah Sheleimah*, 3rd ed., pp. 25-26, comment 134).

3. Since the Exodus story is rich in meaning to both Christian and Jew, any allusion to this theme is bound to automatically carry with it additional connotations. It is, therefore, quite possible that *Le Conte du Graal* was intended to also be interpreted allegorically. As we are in the realm of speculation, I should prefer to *suggest* several possible paths such interpretation might take rather than impose upon the reader any one given interpretation. First let us briefly glance at a strictly Judaic interpretation.

3-A. Professor Holmes had identified the wounded Fisher King with the patriarch Jacob.[13] This biblical character was wounded in the thigh by an angel of God (Genesis 32:26-32). However, his personal redemption as well as that of his entire people was promised him by the Lord (Genesis 28:13-15).

If Professor Holmes was correct in his assumption, Chrétien de Troyes, through his use of *Seder* symbolism may be suggesting that a future redemption awaits the Jews, while simultaneously encouraging Jacob, or the rabbis of Israel, to exert a still greater effort to elicit religious response from their coreligionists (wandering Perceval).

The female Grail Bearer, who, according to Manessier, was a virgin and of the lineage of Israel (i.e., Jacob), is, according to that continuator, the daughter of the Fisher King. She is followed by the female bearer of the carving dish, who is also a virgin and of noble ancestry [14] — the latter is supposedly the daughter of Goot Delsert (variants: Boon Desert and Gondesert), King of the Desert.[15] The juxtaposition of this radiant daughter of Israel with the desert princess might indicate that these figures represent two aspects of the Jewish people — a nation in exile, both in the past (Egypt and the wilderness) and in the present (France). In both cases an optimistic end — Canaan and redemption — await them. In strictly Judaic terms this redemption would be achieved by the advent of the Messiah. However, since a purely Judaic interpretation of the Grail story would be valid only if Chrétien were a converted Jew, as Professor Holmes had suggested, or, if he were directing his message to the Jewish People, it may be

---

[13] *Chrétien, Troyes, and the Grail*, pp. 102-103.

[14] Charles Potvin, ed. *Perceval le Gallois ou le Conte du Graal, publié d'après les manuscrits originaux*, Part II: *Le Poème de Chrétien et de ses continuateurs d'après le manuscrit de Mons* (Mons, 1870), IV, vv. 35167-35173.

[15] *Ibid.*, V, vv. 48003-48004.

more appropriate to interpret the Grail scene as a Christian allegory superimposed upon a Jewish base.

3-B. As the ecclesiastic writings dealing with Exodus are overwhelming in number, it is beyond the scope of these pages to present an exhaustive analysis of the Christian exegetical treatment of the Exodus. It is possible, however, to discern several major directions which such exegesis did take and to suggest possible interpretations for Chrétien's work on the basis of these.

The Church interpreted Scripture as containing, in addition to a literal or historic meaning, "fuller senses" of interpretation. Thus, Garnier of Rochefort (or of Saint-Victor), the 12th-century author of the *Allegoriae in Sacram Scripturam*, explained that "Jerusalem," in addition to its metonymical sense of the inhabitants of that city, signified allegorically the Church in the person of Jesus, tropologically the Soul, and anagogically the habitation of the Heavenly City. [16]

Just as the Jews interpreted the Exodus as a figure for a Messianic advent, the Christians interpreted the pentateuchal Exodus as a figure for a Second Exodus to occur under the sign of Jesus. [17]

Borrowing Garnier's order, let us explore three possible interpretations of *Le Conte du Graal* based upon the following *fuller* Christian interpretations of the Exodus:

(1) The liberation of a Christian people through the sacraments of the Church.

(2) The liberation of an individual soul or of a people through Conversion.

---

[16] *Allegoriae in Sacram Scripturam*, PL CXII, col. 966. This work had been attributed by Migne to Rabanus Maurus. See P[almeon] Glorieux, *Pour revaloriser Migne: Tables rectificatives*, Mélanges de Science Religieuse, IXe Année, Cahier Supplémentaire (Lille, 1952) for this correction.

[17] Indeed, Jesus himself was viewed as the Paschal sacrifice, as a New Israel, and as a Second Moses, and the events of the Exodus were associated with events in his life. See, Jean Daniélou, *Sacramentum Futuri: Etudes sur les origines de la typologie biblique* (Paris, 1950), p. 137; A. C. Charity, *Events and their Afterlife; The Dialectics of Christian Typology in the Bible and Dante* (Cambridge, England, 1966), pp. 103-135; W. D. Davies, *The Setting of the Sermon on the Mount* (Cambridge, 1964), pp. 25-93; Gabriel Hebert, *When Israel Came out of Egypt* (Richmond, [Va.], 1961), pp. 113-115; Louis Pirot and Albert Clamer, eds., *La Sainte Bible, Texte latin et traduction française d'après les textes originaux avec un commentaire exégétique et théologique*, Vol. I, 2° part: *Exode* (Paris, 1956), p. 55.

(3) The life struggle or "Pilgrimage of Life," which a Christian must undertake from a terrestrial Egypt to the Celestial City.

(1) The Church Fathers in their catechistic writings as well as the medieval exegetes interpreted the Exodus as the liberation of Man, or of a Christian people,[18] through the sacraments of the Church.[19]

The crossing of the Red Sea, the cloud, and the rock were seen as figures for Baptism. This analogy, of Pauline origin (I Corinthians 10:2-11), was developed by the Church Fathers and exegetes.[20] Indeed, Baptism itself figures in the Holy Saturday ritual.[21] The water, which issued forth from the rock, was seen as the blood of Jesus and the manna as the Eucharist,[22] Moses and Aaron as Priests,[23] the cloud as the Holy Spirit,[24] and the Jordan, either as a Baptism of the Humbles[25] or as a Second Baptism in Jesus.[26]

---

[18] Zeno Veronensis, *Tractatus*, II, 54 P.L. XI, cols. 509-510.
[19] Tertullianus, *De Baptismo adversus Quintillam Liber VIII, IX*, P.L. I, cols. 1197-1224; Rabanus Maurus, *Commentaria in Exodum*, "Praefatio," P.L. CVIII, col. 9:

> Inter caeteras Scripturas quas Pentateuch legis continet, merite liber Exodi eminet in quo pene omnia sacramenta quibus praesens Ecclesia instituitur, nutritur et regitur, figuraliter exprimuntur. (Cf. Daniélou, *Sacramentum futuri*, pp. 154-155.)

[20] Origenes, *Homiliae in Exodum*, V, VI, P.G. XII cols. 325-340; Didymus Alexandrinus, *De Trinitate*, II, 14, P.G. XXXIX, col. 697; Basilius Magnus, *Liber de Spiritu Sanctu*, XIV, P.G. XXXII, col. 122; Augustinus, *Contra Faustum Manichaeum*, XII, 28-29, P.L. XLII, cols. 269-270; Joannis Chrysostomi "In Dictum Pauli nolo vos ignorari," *Homiliae*, P.G. LI, col. 248; Ambrosius, *De Mysteriis* III, 13, P.L. XVI, col. 393. Pseudo Ambrosius (Nicetas Aquileiensis Episcopus or Venerius de Milano), *De Sacramentis* I, and IV, 12, P.L. XVI, col. 421; Petrus Lombardus, *Collectanea in Omnes D. Pauli Apostoli Epistolas*, P.L. CXCI, col. 1618.
[21] Guillaume Durand, *Rational ou Manuel des divins offices ou raisons mystiques et historiques de la liturgie catholique*, tr. Charles Barthelémy (Paris, 1854), Vol. 4, II, 146-184.
[22] Theodoretus, *Quaestiones in Exodum*, XXVIII, P.G. LXXX, col. 257.
[23] Zeno Veronensis, *Tractatus II*, 54, P.L. XI, col. 509; Cyrillus Archepiscepus Hierosolymitanus, *Catechesis*, XIX, *Mystagogica* I, P.G. XXXIII, col. 1068.
[24] Ambrosius, *De Mysteriis*, III, 13, P.L. XVI, col. 393; Pseudo Ambrosius, *De Sacramentis*, I, VI, 20-22, P.L. XVI, cols. 423-424.
[25] Alanus de Insulis, *Distinctiones Dictionum Theologicalium*, P.L. CCX, col. 823; Petrus Lombardus, *Commentarium in Psalmos*, CXIII, P.L. CXCI, col. 1019; Cf. Durand, *Rational*, p. 167.
[26] Origenes, *Commentaria in Evangelium Joannis*, P.G. XIV, cols. 43-44;

Since Perceval's evolution is towards reception of the sacraments of Penance (6440-6444, 6478-6479), and Communion (6512-6513), so that he may obtain Grace, we may see Perceval, in the words of Augustine, as a figure for "a baptized people, led through the desert, who, though not yet enjoying the Promised Land, aspire toward it" [27] — with the implication that they shall realize this aspiration.

(2) Related to the sacrament of Baptism, implicit in the crossing of the Red Sea and the Jordan, is the theme of Conversion. [28] The Exodus was seen as a sort of initiation into Christianity. The Israelites' hastiness in preparing their meal was seen as the haste of Conversion; [29] their leaving Egypt was interpreted as a break with idolatry; the crossing of the Red Sea was explained as an entrance into the catechisminate, [30] and Jerusalem was seen as the triumph of the Church [31] or the presence of the Jesus diffused over the entire world. [32]

Commentaries on the 113th Psalm ("In Exitu Israel de Aegypto") reiterated the Exodus-Conversion motif, [33] stressing, in particular, the

---

Homiliae in Librum Jesu Nave, I, 3, P.G. XII, col. 828; Gregorius Episcopus Nysseni; *Adversus eos qui Baptismum different*, P.G. XLVI, cols. 420-421; *In Baptismum Christi*, P.G. XLVI, col. 592.

[27] Augustinus, *Contra Faustum Manichaeum*, XII, P.L. XLII, col. 270.

[28] See Rudolf Bultmann, "Prophesy and Fulfillment," *Essays on Old Testament Hermaneutics*, ed. Claus Westermann, tr. James Luther Mays (Richmond, Va., 1963), p. 52; E. Johnson, "Easter and its Cycle," *New Catholic Encyclopedia*, ed. Catholic University of America (New York, 1967), V, 6-9; A. C. Charity, *Events and their Afterlife: The Dialectics of Christian Typology in the Bible and Dante* (Cambridge England, 1966), p. 161. Charles S. Singleton, "*In Exitu Israel de Aegypto*," *Dante: A Collection of Critical Essays*, ed., John Freccero (Englewood Cliffs, N.J., 1965), pp. 102-121.

[29] Richard de Saint-Victor (Pseudo Hugo de S. Victore), "*Allegoriae in Vetus Testamentum*," P.L. CLXXV, col. 655.

[30] Daniélou *Sacramentum futuri*, p. 240.

[31] Alanus de Insulis, *Distinctiones Dictionum Theologicalium*, P.L. CCX, cols. 822-823.

[32] Garnier de Rochefort or de Saint-Victor (Pseudo Rabanus Maurus), *Allegoriae in Sacram Scripturam*, P.L. CXII, col. 996.

[33] E.g. Petrus Lombardus, *Commentarium in Psalmos*, Psalm 113, verse 5, P.L. CXCI, cols. 1019-1020; Alanus de Insulis, *Distinctiones Dictionum Theologicalium*, P.L. CCX, col. 823; Cf. Anselmus Laudunensis (Pseudo Walafridus Strabus), *Glossa Ordinaria* (Psalm 113, verse 3), P.L. CXIII, col. 1035:

> *Vidit mare,* id est peccatores saeculi. *Jordanis,* qui variis desideriis rapiunt homines in magnum mare, id est hujus saeculi amaricantem malitiam; sed haec in adventu Domini cessant quasi conversa retrorsum.

conversion of the Jews.[34] The Exodus imagery of I Corinthians 10:1-3 was similarly interpreted.[35]

If we then view the Grail episode from this perspective, Perceval, who wanders through the desert, might represent the Errant Jew. Due to his obstinacy and egotism (i.e., his naive and unfaltering belief in the sole validity of the Old Law), he had rejected, or failed to understand his mother's lessons about Jesus. At the Fisher King's castle he is, for the same reeson, unable to ask the questions that would bring about his own redemption or that of the Fisher King's (Jacob's) realm. But even had he succeeded at that time in asking the proper questions, he would have been unable to comprehend the answers to them (the allusion to the Passion implicit in the description of the host carried on the grail, or perhaps the Exodus story with its message of conversion). It is only after experiencing great personal suffering and prolonged exile that he will be able to repent and finally accept Jesus (i.e., arrive at the Promised Land). The two maidens (according to their presentation in the Manessier continuation) might then symbolize two aspects of the people of Israel — a nation presently wandering in the desert, but who in the future, as newly converted Christians, will arrive at the Promised Land.

Since the Exodus-Conversion figure applies with equal validity to the personal religious commitments of Christians, an alternate Judeo-Christian reading of *Le Conte du Graal* might view the narrative as directed entirely toward Christians or more specifically toward the knightly class, exhorting its members to re-examine their conduct and rededicate their chivalric pursuits toward Christian ends.

(3) The Entry of the Chosen People into the Promised Land was also viewed as a prefiguration for a "pilgrimage of life." The Christians were seen as the "strangers and pilgrims" of Hebrews 11:13, Leviticus 25:13, and Psalms 39:12, headed towards a "better country" (Hebrews 11:13), a heavenly Jerusalem [36] or Kingdom of

---

[34] Anselmus Laudunensis (Pseudo Walafridus Strabus), *Glossa Ordinaria* (Psalm 113, verse 8), P.L. CXIII, col. 1035; *Qui convertit petram,* ... dura corda Judaeorum, ad aquam baptismi.

[35] See Gabriel Hebert (*When Israel Came out of Egypt* [Richmond, Va., 1961], p. 113) for mention of the analogy between these verses and the "cloud of divine presence" at the time of conversion and baptism.

[36] Philippians 3:20; Cf. Hebrews 11:11-16, Luke 10:30-36. See Samuel C. Chew, *The Pilgrimage of Life* (New Haven, 1962), pp. 174-175.

Jesus.[37] Richard of Saint-Victor interpreted the Exodus by giving a minute description of such a spiritual pilgrimage:

> Arma quibus filii Israel leguntur armati, virtutes insinuant quibus contra vitia armarmur, castitatem per quam munimur contra luxuriam, humilitatem contra superbiam et sic de caeteris virtutibus et vitiis. Farina non fermentata quam secum tulerunt, simplicem et sanam doctrinam designat. Mare Rubrum baptismum significat Christi sanguine consecretum.... Desertum quod transito Mari Rubrae filii Israel intraverunt, vitam significat spiritualem quam accepta baptismi gratia agere debemus.... Amalecitae qui primu filiis Israel armati occurererunt et reges qui postea contra eos pugnaverunt duorum vitiorum demonstrant carnalia et spiritualia cum duplici hoste pugnantia per diversos homines et daemones.... Jordanus, qui interpretatur *descensus* significat mortem: terra promissionis aeternam beatudinem.... Aegyptum itaque vita saecularis desertum vita spiritualis terra promissionis vita coelestis.[38]

Samuel C. Chew formulated a handy working model which we shall adopt for the purposes of this study:

> Man, having through sin forfeited the boon of immortality, passes into the world of time, governed under God's ordinance by Fortune. A free agent, he may choose either of two paths. If he chooses aright, there are perils along the strait and narrow way, but clad in the armor of St. Paul he will be able to withstand the assaults of the Infernal Trinity and though the Deadly Sins assail him a great company of Virtues counsel and protect him. Death awaits him at the journey's end but beyond death the Celestial City.[39]

If we interpret *Le Conte du Graal* in this context, Chrétien's work would be an allegorical "pilgrimage manual" of sorts, whose

---

[37] Gabriel Hebert, *When Israel came out of Egypt* (Richmond Va., 1961), p. 114. Cf. Garnier de Rochefort or de Saint-Victor, *Allegoriae in Sacram Scripturam*, P.L. CXII, col. 966.

[38] Richard de Saint-Victor, *Allegoriae in Vetus Testamentum*, P.L. CLXXV, cols. 655-666.

[39] Samuel C. Chew, *The Pilgrimage of Life*, p. xxiii. Cf. Juan Bautista Avalle-Arce's edition of Cervantes' *Los Trabajos de Persiles y Sigismunda* ([Madrid, 1969], pp. 23-27) for a discussion of the pilgrimages of life and of love in Dante and Cervantes.

intent would be not unlike that of Jerome's *Peregrinatio Sanctae Paulae* and *Epistola ad Marcellam,* or the *Itinerarium Egeriae.* In these works the emotional quality of the descriptions afforded the reader a greater opportunity for personal involvement with the holy places, than did purely historical or geographical accounts of the sacred sites.[40]

If we trace our hero's "pilgrimage" according to this "roadmap," Perceval, through his disobedience (his having abandoned his mother) would enter into the great, dark forest or "desert of life" ("Par un desert aloit" [6239]) governed by Fortuna. This goddess who renders mighty rulers low and humble,[41] may have been responsible for the abject condition of Arthur's realm, described at the outset of the romance — a state in which the "best had fallen" and in which "evil, shame, and sloth" reigned (427-434). Fortuna's presence may likewise

---

[40] Stephen G. Nichols, Jr., "The Interaction of Life and Literature in the *Peregrinationes ad Loca Sancta* and the *Chansons de geste,*" *Speculum,* XLIV (1969), 55-56, 61-62, 71-72. For descriptions of Renaissance allegorical pilgrimages and their iconography, see Chew, *The Pilgrimage of Life,* pp. 174-213.

[41] Boethius, *De Consolatione philosophiae libri quinque cum notis et interpretatione in usum Delphini variis lectionibus notis variorum recensu editionum et codicum et indice locupletissimo* (London, 1823), pp. 155-156:

> Haic cum superba veterit vices dextra
> Et aestuantis more fertur Euripi
> Dudum tremendos saeva proterit reges
> Humilemque victi sublevat fallax vultum.

Hildebertus Cenomanensis, *De Exsilio Suo,* P.L. CLXXI, col. 1419:

> Quidquid habes hodie, cras fortasse relinquet,
> Aut modo dum loqueris desinet esse tuum.
> Ilas ludit fortuna vices, regesque superbos,
> Aut servos humiles non sinit esse diu.

Cf. *Floire et Blancheflor, poème du XIIIe siècle, publié d'après les manuscrits,* ed. M. Edélestand Du Méril (Paris, 1856), vv. 2258-2259; Chrétien de Troyes, *Les Romans de Chrétien de Troyes, édités d'après la copie de Guiot* (Bibl. Nat. fr. 794), Vol. III: *Le Chevalier de la charrette,* ed. Mario Roques, CFMA, No. 86 (Paris, 1958), vv. 5720-5765; Boccaccio, *De Casibus Illustrium Virorum, A Facsimile Reproduction of the Paris Edition of 1520 with an Introduction,* ed. Louis Brewer Hall (Gainesville [Fla.], 1912), II, 13-14, pp. 58-60. The "fall of princes" motif was graphically expressed by the four-part epithet "*regnabo, regno, regnavi, sum sine regno.*" This maxim was illustrated by medieval artists (Howard Patch, *The Goddess Fortuna in Mediaeval Literature* [Cambridge (Mass.), 1927], pp. 59-68; and Alexandre Du Sommerand, *Les Arts au Moyen Age,* Album of Plates. Vol. II, Series 4 [Paris, 1838], plates 38-39).

explain the maritime setting of the Fisher King's castle — its location beyond a mountain in the vicinity of a swiftly flowing body of water, its accessibility via a drawbridge, and the Fisher King's presence upon a boat (2976-3084) — as well the desolation destined to befall this realm.

According to Alain de Lisle, Fortuna's abode is to be found on and island. It is situated partially on a lofty mountain and partially in a valley. It contains both blossoming and barren trees, sweet and bitter plants, and it is both richly and poorly furnished.[42] Nicole de Margival elaborates upon this double image of fertility and desolation associated with Fortuna's dwelling place:

> Mais moult belle est d'une partie
> Et noble et de tous biens garnie;
> De l'autre partie est si gaste
> Que nul n'i a ne pain ne paste,
> Et est ruïneuse et deserte.[43]

These states closely resemble the two conditions, one of which, dependent upon whether or not Perceval would ask the questions, was destined to befall the Fisher King's realm. Aeneas Sylvius adds that concrete walls surround Fortuna's castle and one must pass over a drawbridge to gain access to it.[44] The metaphor of Fortune guiding a craft over the sea of life, is, of course, a commonplace in classical and medieval literature.[45] However, the fact that in Chrétien's text the Fisher King's craft is *anchored* (3006) may indicate to the reader from the very first moment that this man has placed his hope in the Lord[46] — a hope which Perceval, who believes in the infallibility of

---

[42] Alanus de Insulis, *Anticlaudianus sive de Officio Viri Boni et Perfecti*, P.L. CCX, cols. 557-560. Cf. Jean de Meun, *Le Roman de la rose*, ed. Félix Lecoy, CFMA (Paris, 1965), Vol. I, vv. 5891-6102.

[43] Nicole de Margival, *Le Dit de la panthère d'amours, poème du XIIIe siècle, publié d'après les manuscrits de Paris et de Saint Pétersbourg*, ed. Henry A. Todd (Paris, 1883), vv. 1966-1970.

[44] Aeneas Sylvius, Pont. Epist I, cviii, *Opera Omnia* (Basil, 1571), p. 611.

[45] See, for example, Boethius, *De Consolatione Philosophiae* II, prosa iv and note f, p. 176, metra ii, pp. 162-164, and metra iii, p. 171; Hildebertus Cenomanensis, *De Exsilio Suo*, P.L. CLXXI, col. 1419; Cf. Chew, *The Pilgrimage of Life*, pp. 100-113.

[46] Hebrews 6:19: "Here [in the hope held out to us] we have a firm anchor for our soul."

arms, does not yet share. Perceval's admittance to the Grail Castle, however, is in itself an optimistic sign since few are permitted to even enter Fortuna's domain.[47]

In Chrétien's text, the comely Grail Bearer and the Loathly Damsel may be representations of two aspects of the goddess Fortuna who traditionally possessed two guises: that of a beautiful young maiden, and that of a ravaged, hideous old lady.[48] This feminine figure would bestow royal favors at will.[49] The goddess Fortuna was, furthermore, often associated with Occasio, the goddess of the opportune moment, whose standard image was that of a bald woman with a forelock (which was presumably to be seized before she passes by).[50] The Loathly Damsel's exclamation:

> "Ha! Perchevaux, Fortune [est] cauve
> Detriers et devant chavelue.
> Et dehais ait qui te salue
> Ne qui nul bien t'ore ne prie,
> Que tu ne la recheüs mie
> Fortune quant tu l'encontras," (4646-4651)

---

[47] Brassenex (Watriquet) de Couvin, "*Dis de l'Escharbote*," vv. 83-86, *Dits de Watriquet de Couvin, publiés d'après les manuscrits de Paris et de Bruxelles et accompagnés de notes explicatives*, ed. Auguste Scheler (Brussels, 1868), p. 400; Aeneas Sylvius, Pontif. Epist. I, cviii, *Opera Omnia*, p. 611. Cf. Howard Patch, *The Goddess Fortuna in Mediaeval Literature*, p. 611.

[48] Boethius, *De Consolatione Philosophiae*, II, prosa i, pp. 149-155; Boccaccio, *De Casibus Illustrium Virorum*, IV, 1, p. 141. Cf. Chew (*The Pilgrimage of Life*, pp. 36-43) who cites descriptions by Augustine and Petrarch; and Patch, *The Goddess Fortuna in Mediaeval Literature*, pp. 36-43.

[49] Boethius, *De Consolatione Philosophiae*, II, metrum i, pp. 156-157; Hildebertus Cenomanensis, *De Exsilio Suo*, P.L. CLXXI, col. 1419. Cf. Patch, *The Goddess Fortuna in Mediaeval Literature*, p. 59.

[50] This image, first found in the *Distichs* of Cato, which was highly popular in the Middle Ages, was rendered into French by several authors, among them Elie de Wincestre. The common confusion of Occasio with Fortuna stems from a substitution which Evrand made in his version of the *Distichs*. For more details concerning this image see J. E. Matzke, "On the Source of the Italian and English Idioms meaning 'To take Time by the Forelock'," *PMLA*, VIII (1893), 303-334; George Lyman Kittredge, "To take Time by the Forelock," *Modern Language Notes*, VIII (1893), 230-235; Karl Pietsch, "On the Source of 'To take Time by the Forelock'," *Modern Language Notes*, VIII (1893), 235-338. For the iconography of Occasio see Chew, *The Pilgrimage of Life*, p. 26, and Patch, *The Goddess Fortuna in Mediaeval Literature*, p. 114.

by which she rebukes Perceval for not having seized Fortuna (here confused with Occasio) while at the Grail Castle, may suggest a relationship between herself, the Grail Bearer, and Fortuna-Occasio.

The two paths which Perceval sees before him after the Loathly Damsel's visit — the one paved with fame and honor, the other with hardship (4688-4746) — are not unlike those of the "pilgrimage of life" described in Matthew 7: 13-14: the one, "wide and broad," leading to destruction, the other, "strait and narrow," leading to life. [51]

Perceval (symbolic of the individual Christian) had, during the course of his "pilgrimage," been assailed by and succumbed to the Infernal Trinity — sins of the Devil (his Pride, in placing arms above religion), sins of the World (his Envy of the knights, and his Wrath in the murder of the Red Knight and his choleric disposition following his first encounter with the Fisher King before approaching the Grail Castle), and sins of the Flesh (Gluttony, in his repeated concern for his stomach, and Lechery, personified, perhaps, by Blancheflor). However, after disarming himself at the hermitage (6339), Perceval, through his humility and penance, will convert the arms which he initially obtained from the Red Knight and later received official sanction to wear from Gornemant (his halbert, spurs, shield, helmet, and sword [1176-1191, 1624-1638]) to the Pauline armor of Ephesians 6: 13-18: the girdle of Truth, the breastplate of Righteousness, the footwear of preparation of the Gospel of Peace, the shield of Faith, helmet of Salvation, and sword of the Spirit. Perceval, as a *miles Christi*, will now presumably overcome the vices which assail him, and will, as did the Israelites, successfully cross the Jordan. Gaining the salvation foretold at the outset of the romance when the Red Knight's helmet became him well (1182), Perceval will, upon the completion of his "pilgrimage," enter into the Celestial City.

* * * * *

---

[51] These two paths were often iconographically represented by the Pythagorean "Y". See Chew, *The Pilgrimage of Life,* pp. 174-178.

PLATE 13. Procession with Symbolic Passover Foods. *Haggadah, British Museum Add. 14761.* 14th Century, Spanish.

INTERPRETATION AND CONCLUSIONS

Since literary interpretation, as beauty, is in the eye of the beholder, my intent in this chapter has not been to deprive the reader of his own creativity by imposing upon him *ex cathedra* any one allegorical interpretation for *Le Conte du Graal*. My desire was rather to suggest several paths which such interpretation may follow when viewed from the perspective of the *Seder*.

But regardless of how one chooses to interpret the basic *Seder* imagery of Chrétien's Grail episode, I am convinced that it is impossible to find another theory capable of explaining as many mysteries of the Grail Castle while at the same time being based upon as compact and as unified a corpus of source material.

Considering the extensive contact between Christian and Jew during medieval times, an examination of Jewish sources may, in the future, prove to be both an interesting and fruitful point of departure in a serious study of the themes, imagery, and symbolism of other literary works of this period.

BIBLIOGRAPHY

Texts

Abudarham, David ben Yoseph. *Peirush Haberakhot Vehatephilot Abudarham Hashalem.* Jerusalem, 1958.

———. *Sepher Abudarham.* ed. Rabbi M. A. Kempler. Brooklyn, n.d.

Aeneas Sylvius. *Opera Omnia.* Basel, 1571.

Alanus de Insulis. *Anticlaudianus, sive de Officio Viri Boni et Perfecti Libri IX.* P.L. CCX. 482-578.

———. *Distinctiones Dictionum Theologicalium.* P.L. CCX, 635-1021.

Ambrosius. *De Mysteriis Liber.* P.L. XVI, 367-416.

Pseudo Ambrosius (Nicetas Aquileiensis Episcopus or Venerius de Milan). *De Sacramentis Libri Sex.* P.L. XVI, 417-464.

Anonymous. "Kol Bo," *Haggadah shel Pesaḥ im Meah Veḥamishah Asar Peirushim.* ed. Yisrael Miller. Jerusalem?, 196?.

Anselmus Laudunensis (Pseudo Walafridus Strabus). *Glossa Ordinaria.* P.L. CXIII and CXIV.

Augustinus. *Contra Faustum Manichaeum Libri XXXIII.* P.L. XLII, 207-518.

Babylonian Talmud. *Tractate Pesaḥim.* Vilna, 1886.

Baile in Scáil. "Baile in Scail," ed. R. Thurneysen, *Zeitschrift für celtische Philologie und Volksforschung,* XII (1918), 239-250.

———. "Der Anfang von Baile in Scail," ed. Julius Pokerny, *Zeitschrift für celtische Philologie,* XIII (1921), 317-382.

Basilius Magnus. *Liber de Spiritu Sancto.* P.G. XXXII, 67-218.

Benjamin [ben Jonah] of Tudela. *The Itinerary of Benjamin of Tudela. Critical Text, Translation, and Commentary.* tr. and ed. Marcus Nathan Adler. London, 1907.

———. "The Travels of Rabbi Benjamin of Tudela, 1160-1173," tr. Thomas Wright, *Contemporaries of Marco Polo, Consisting of the Travel Records to The Eastern Parts of the World of William Rubruck (1253-1255); The Journey of John of Pian de Carpini (1245-1247); The Journal of Friar Odoric (1318-1330) and The Oriental Travels of Rabbi Benjamin of Tudela (1160-1173),* ed. Manuel Komroff. New York, 1928.

Bible.

    Dhorme, Edouard; Koenig, Jean; Michaeli, Frank; Hadot, Jean; and Guillaumot, Antoine; trs. and eds. *L'Ancien Testament*, Vols. I and II. Paris, 1956-1959.

    Ecole Biblique de Jérusalem. *La Sainte Bible, traduite en français sous la direction de l'Ecole Biblique de Jérusalem.* Paris, 1961.

    Jones, Alexender, ed. *The Jerusalem Bible.* Garden City, New York, 1966.

    Leteris, Meir Halevi, ed. and Leeser, Isaac, tr. *The Hebrew Bible: Sepher Torah Neviim Uketuvim.* New York, 1926.

    Pirot, Louis and Clamer, Albert trs. and eds. *La Sainte Bible. Texte latin et traduction française d'après les textes originaux avec un commentaire exégétique et théologique.* Tome I, 2ᵉ Partie: Exode. Paris, 1956.

    Rosenbaum, M., and Silberman, A. M., trs. *Pentateuch with Targum Onkelos, Haphtaroth and Prayers for the Sabbath and Rashi's Commentary.* 5 vols. London, 1946.

Boccaccio, Giovanni. *De Casibus Illustrium Virorum. A Facsimile Reproduction of the Paris Edition of 1520,* ed. Louis Brewer Hall. Gainesville, Florida, 1962.

Boethius. *De Consolatione Philosophiae Libri Quinque Ex Editione Vulpiana cum Notis et Interpretatione in Usum Delphini Variis Lectionibus Notis Variorum Recensu Editionum et Codicum,* Scriptores Latini in Usum Delphini, XVI. London, 1823.

Brassenex (Watriquet) de Couvin. *Dits de Watriquet de Couvin publiés d'après les manuscrits de Paris et de Bruxelles et accompagnés de variantes et de notes explicatives,* ed. Auguste Scheler. Brussels, 1868.

Cath Maige Tured. "Die zweite Schlacht von Mag Tured und die keltische Götterlehre," ed. Lehmacher, Gustav, S. J., *Anthropos,* XXVI (1931), 435-459.

Cervantes, Miguel de. *Los Trabajos de Persiles y Sigismunda. Edición, introducción y notas,* ed. Juan Bautista Avalle-Arce. Madrid, 1969.

Chrétien de Troyes. *Les Romans de Chrétien de Troyes édités d'après la copie de Guiot.* (Bibl. Nat., fr. 794), Vol. I: *Erec et Enide,* ed. Mario Roques. CFMA, LXXX. Paris, 1953. Vol. II: *Cligès,* ed. Alexandre Micha. CFMA, LXXXIV. Paris, 1957. Vol. III: *Le Chevalier de la charrette,* ed. Mario Roques. CFMA, LXXXVI. Paris, 1958. Vol. IV: *Le Chevalier au Lyon* (Yvain), ed. Mario Roques. CFMA, LXXXIX. Paris, 1960.

Chrétien de Troyes. *Erec und Enide,* ed. Wendelin Foerster, 3rd ed. Romanische Bibliothek, XIII. Halle, 1934.

―――. *Le Roman de Perceval ou le Conte du Graal,* ed. William Roach, 2nd ed. Textes Littéraires Français. LXXI. Geneva, 1959.

―――. *Christian von Troyes sämtliche erhaltene Werke,* V: *Der Percevalroman (Li Contes del Graal),* ed. Alfons Hilka. Halle, 1932.

―――. *Perceval le Gallois ou Le Conte du Graal publié d'après les manuscrits originaux,* Deuxième Partie, Vols. I and II: *Le Poème de Chrétien de Troyes et de ses continuateurs d'après le manuscrit de Mons,* ed. Ch[arles] Potvin. Société des Bibliophiles Belges, Publication XXI. 6 vols. Mons, 1866-67.

Chrétien de Troyes. *Perceval le Gallois ou le Conte du Graal,* tr. Lucien Foulet. Paris, 1947.
———. *The Story of the Grail,* tr. Robert White Linker. Chapel Hill, 1952.
———. *Perceval, or the Story of the Grail by Chrétien de Troyes,* trs. Roger Sherman Loomis and Laura Hibbard Loomis, in *Medieval Romances.* New York, 1957.
Pseudo Cyprianus (Sixtus II?) *Tractatus adversus Judaeos.* P.L. IV, 919-924.
Cyrillus, Archepiscopus Hierosolymitanus. *Catachesis.* P.G. XXXIII, 331-1058. *Catachesis Mystagogicae Quinque.* P.G. XXXIII, 1059-1131.
Didymus Alexandrinus. *De Trinitate.* P.G. XXXIX, 269-991.
Durand, Guillaume. *Rational ou Manuel des divins offices ou raisons mystiques et historiques de la liturgie catholique,* tr. M. Charles Barthelémy. Vol. IV. Paris, 1854.
Eisenstein, J. D., ed. *Otzar Peirushim Vetziyurim el Haggadah shel Pesaḥ. A compendium (in Hebrew) of Authoritative Commentaries and Original Illustrations on the Hagada.* New York, 1920.
Floire et Blancheflor; poème du XIIIe siècle publié d'après les manuscrits, ed. Edélestand Du Méril. Paris, 1856.
Garnier de Rochefort or de Saint-Victor (Pseudo Rabanus Maurus). *Allegoriae in Sacram Scripturam.* P.L. CXII, 842-1088.
Giraldus, Cambrensis. *Gemma Ecclesiastica,* in *Opera,* ed. J. S. Brewer. London, 1862. II.
Gregorius Episcopus Nysseni. *Adversus Eos qui Baptismum Differunt.* P.G. XLVI, 415-434.
———. *In Baptismum Christi.* P.G. XLVI, 577-598.
Guillaume de Lorris et Jean de Meun. *Le Roman de la Rose,* ed. Félix Lecoy. 3 vols., Les Classiques Français du Moyen Age. Paris, 1965-1970.
———. *Le Roman de la Rose par Guillaume de Lorris et Jehan de Meung,* ed. D.M. Méon, 4 vols. Paris, 1814.

Haggadah.

>   Berdah, Davis, tr. *La Haggadah de Pâque avec traduction et commentaires en langue française.* Tunis, 1957.
>   Belforto, Shelomoh, et. al. *Sepher Moadei Hashem Keminhag Kahal Kadosh Sephardim.* Leghorn, 1862.
>   Eherenreich, Shelomo Zalman, ed. *Haggadah shel Pesaḥ im Peirush Afikoman Upeirush Matzah Sheleimah.* Jerusalem, 196?.
>   Goldschmidt, E. D[aniel]. *The Passover Haggadah: Its Sources and History* (in Hebrew). Jerusalem, 1960.
>   *Haggadah shel Pesaḥ Kephi Minhag Hasephardim V. Tz. V. Estampada con letra hermosa y ladinada.* Vienna: Schlesinger, n.d.
>   Ḥutsin, Shelomoh Bekhor, tr. and ed. *Seder Haggadah shel Pesaḥ im Srah Aravi Vetargum Aravi Kephi Minhag K.K. Bagdad.* Leghorn, 1867.
>   Italiener, Bruno; Freinmann, Aron; Mayer, August N.; and Schmidt, Adolf. *Die Darmstaedter Pessach Haggadah, Codex orientalis 8 der Landesbibliothek zu Darmstadt.* Leipzig, 1927.
>   Kapeḥ, Yoseph, ed. *Sepher Agadeta Depesaḥ Keminhag Olei Teiman im Arbaah Mephorshim.* Jerusalem, 1959.

Kasher, Menaḥem M. and Ashkenazi, Shemuel, eds. *Haggadah Sheleimah*. Jerusalem, 1961. 3rd ed. Jerusalem, 1967.
Kasher, Menaḥem M., ed. *Israel Passover Haggadah*. tr. Aaron Greenbaum. New York, 1964.
Leeser, Isaac, ed. *The Form of Prayers according to the Custom of the Spanish and Portuguese Jews*. 2nd ed., Vol. V. Philadelphia, 1953.
Miller, Yisrael David, ed. *Haggadah shel Pesaḥ im Meah Veḥamishah Asar Peirushim*. Jerusalem?, 196?.
Neiman, Shimon Betzalel, ed. *Haggadah shel Pesaḥ im Peirush Yalkut Shimoni*. Jerusalem, 1965-66.
Nerson, Robert. *La Haggada commentée: traduction et commentaire du texte intégral de la Haggada de Pâque; explication des usages du sédère*. Paris, 1966.
Oriental Library of the Hungarian Academy of Sciences. *The Kaufman Haggada. Facsimile ed. of Ms 422 of the Kaufmann Collection in the Oriental Library of the Hungarian Academy of Sciences* (Magyar tudományos akadémia, Budapest, Könyutar). Publications of the Oriental Library, I. Budapest, 1957.
Roth, Cecil, tr. and ed. *Haggada for Passover copied and illustrated by Ben Shahn with a Translation, Introduction and Historical Notes by Cecil Roth*. New York and Paris, 1965.
Roth, Cecil. "The John Rylands Haggadah," *John Rylands Library Manchester Bulletin*, XLIII (1960-61), 131-159.
Roth, Cecil, ed. *The Sarajevo Haggadah* (facsimile edition). New York, 1965?.
Saadya ben Yoseph. *Siddur R. Saadya Gaon, Kitab Gami Aṣ-ṣalawāt Wat-tasābiḥ*, eds. I. Davidson, S. Assaf, B. I. Joel. Jerusalem, 1963.
Schneerson, M., ed. *Sepher Otzar Haḥasidim Haggadah shel Pesaḥ Likutei Taamim Uminhagim*. Brooklyn, New York, 1960.
Hayarḥi, Rabbi Avraham ben Rabbi Natan of Lunel. *Sepher Hamanhig, Kolel Teamei Viysodei Khol Haminhagim, Dinim Vehalakhot*. Jerusalem, 1967.
Helinandus Frigidi Montis Monachis. *Chronicon*, P.L. CCXII, 771-1082.
Hildebertus Cenomanensis Episcopus. Deinde Turonensis Archiepiscopus. *De Exsilio Suo*. P.L. CLXXI, 1419-1458.
Ibn Hazm, Ali. *The Dove's Neck-Ring*, tr. A. R. Nykl. Paris, 1931.
Joannis Chrysostomi, "In Dictum Pauli Nolo vos Ignorare etc.," *Homiliae XXV in Quaedam Loca Novi Testamenti*. P.G. LI, 242-252.
Karo, Yoseph. *Shulḥan Arukh im kol Hamephorshim Kaasher Nidpas Mikedem veim Hosaphot Ḥadashot*, Vol. I: *Oraḥ Ḥayyim*. Brooklyn, 1965 or 1966.
Kimḥi, David. *Sepher Hashorashim... Vehu Ḥelek Misepher Hamikhlol... Thesaurus Linguae Sanctae sive Dictionarium Hebreum*, ed. Eliyahu Halevi. Venice: Marco Antonio Justinian, 1547.
———. *Otzar Lashon Hakodesh. Thesaurus Linguae Sanctae ex R. David Kimchi. Sepher Hashorashim*, ed. Sanctus Pagninus Lucensi. Naples: Robertus Stephanus, 1548.
Les Mabinogion, tr. J. Loth. Paris, 1889. I.
The Mabinogion, tr. Charlotte Guest. London and Toronto, 1919.

The Mabinogion, tr. Gwyn Jones and Thomas Jones. London and New York, 1963.
The Mabinogion, tr. W. S. Gruffydd. Transactions of the Hon. Soc. of Cymmrodorion. London, 1914.
Le Ménagier de Paris, traité de morale et d'économie domestique composé vers 1393 par un Parisien. Société de Bibliophiles français. 2 vols. Paris, 1846.
Midrash Rabah al Ḥamishah Ḥumshei Torah Veḥamesh Megilot im Peirushim Matanot Kehunah Veaseiphat Omrim. Vol. II: *Midrash Rabah al Sepher Shemot Umegilat Ester.* Jerusalem, 1965.
Nicole de Margival. *Le Dit de la panthère d'amours par Nicole de Margival, poème du XIII*ᵉ *siècle publié d'après les manuscrits de Paris et Saint Pétersbourg,* ed. Henry A. Todd. Société des Anciens Textes Français. Paris, 1883.
Origenes. *Commentaria in Evangelium Joannis.* P.G. XIV, 21-740.
———. *Homiliae in Exodum.* P.G. XII, 263-393.
———. *Homiliae in Librum Jesu Nave.* P.G. XII, 825-948.

Perceval.

  Perceval le Gallois ou le Conte du Graal, publié d'après les manuscrits originaux.
  Part One: *Le Roman en Prose de la fin du XII*ᵉ *siècle,* ed. Ch[arles] Potvin. Société des Bibliophiles Belges. Mons, 1886.
  Part Two: *Le Poème de Chrétien et de ses continuateurs d'après le manuscrit de Mons,* ed. Ch[arles] Potvin, 5 vols. Société des Bibliophiles Belges. Mons, 1866-1871.
  The Continuations of the Old French Perceval of Chrétien de Troyes, ed. William Roach. 3 vols. Philadelphia, 1955.

Petrus Lombardus. *Collectanea in Omnes D. Pauli Apostoli Epistolas.* P.L. CXCI, 1297-1694.
———. *Commentarium in Psalmos.* P.L. CXCI, 31-1296.
Petrus Venerabilis. (Pseudo William of Champeaux). *Tractatus adversus Judaeorum Inveteratam Duritiem,* P.L. CLXXXIX, 507-657.
. Petrus Blesensis. *Liber contra Perfidiam Judaeorum,* P.L. CCVII, 825-870.
Rabanus Maurus. *Commentaria in Exodum.* P.L. CVIII, 9-248.
Radbertus Paschasius. *De Corpore et Sanguine Domini,* P.L. CXXX, 1351-1497.
Rashi, Rabbi Shelomoh ben Yitzḥak of Troyes. *Sepher Pardes Hagadol Vesepher Haorah,* eds. Mikhael Levi Frumkin and Yitzḥak Finkelstein. Warsaw, 1870. [Jerusalem]: Mephitzei Or [1959].
Richard de Saint-Victor (Pseudo Hugo de S. Victore). *Allegoriae in Vetus Testamentum,* P.L. CLXXV, 635-750.
———. "De Absalon significante Judaeos," *Sermones Centum,* P.L. CLXXVII, 1077-1081.
Robert de Boron. *Le Roman de l'Estoire dou Graal,* ed. William A. Nitze. Paris, 1927.
Roman d'Alexandre. *The Medieval French Roman d'Alexandre.* Vol. I: *Text of the Arsenal and Venice Versions,* ed. M. S. LaDu. Elliott Monographs in the Romance Languages and Literatures, XXXVI. Princeton and Paris, 1937. Vol. II: Version of *Alexandre de Paris,* eds. E. C. Armstrong,

D. L. Buffum, Bateman Edwards, and L. F. H. Lowe. Elliott Monographs, xxxvii. Princeton and Paris, 1937. Vol. III: Version of *Alexandre de Paris*: Variants and Notes to Branch I, ed. Alfred Foulet. Elliott Monographs, xxxviii. Princeton, 1949.
Rupertus Abbas Tuitiensis. *Annulus sive Dialogus Inter Christianum et Judaeum*, P.L. CLXX, 559-608.
Saadya ben Yoseph. *Siddur R. Saadya Gaon, Kitāb Gami' Aṣ-ṣalawāt Wattasābiḥ*, eds. I. Davidson, S. Assaf, B.I. Joel. Jerusalem, 1963.
Shimon bar Tzemaḥ. *Matzah Sheleimah*, in *Haggadah shel Pesaḥ im Peirush Afikoman Upeirush Matzah Sheleimah*, ed. Shelomoh Zalman Eherinreich. Jerusalem, 196?.
Simḥah ben Shemuel of Vitry, Rabbi. *Maḥzor Vitry*, ed. Shimon Halevi Horowitz. Jerusalem, 1963.
Skene, William Forbes, ed. *The Four Ancient Books of Wales*, 2 vols. Edinburgh, 1862.
Tertullianus. *De Baptismo adversus Quintillam Liber*. P.L. I, 1197-1224.
Theodoretus *Quaestiones in Exodum*. P.G. LXXX, 225-400.
Tuirell Bicrenn. "Tuirell Bicrenn und seine Kinder," ed. R. Thurneysen, *Zeitschrift für celtische Philologie und Volksforschung*, XII (1918), 239-250.
Yonah ibn Janaḥ. *The Book of Hebrew Roots of Abu'l Walīd ibn Janâh, called Rabbi Jônâh. Edited with an Appendix containing Extracts from other Hebrew Arabic Dictionnaries with Additions and Corrections by Wilhelm Bacher*, ed. Adolf Neubauer. Amsterdam, 1968. Reprint of the Edition of Oxford, 1875.
Zeno Veronensis. *Tractatus*. P.L. XI, 253-526.

Critical Studies

Abrahams, I. "Some Egyptian Fragments of the Passover Haggadah," *Jewish Quarterly Review*, X (1898), 46-47.
Adolf, Helen. "The Esplumoir Merlin," *Speculum*, XXI (1946), 173-193.
Amadi, Yitzḥak. "*Miminhagei Yahadut Kurdistan*," *Yalkut Minhagim*, ed. Avraham Ben Yaakov. Jerusalem, 1967, pp. 43-73.
Anitchkof, Eugène. "Le Saint Graal et les rites eucharistiques," *Romania*, LV (1929), 174-194.
Bacher, W. "Abraham ibn Ezra dans le nord de la France," *Revue des Etudes Juives*, XVII (1896), 300-304.
Barukh, Y. L., and Levinsky, Yom-Tov. *Sepher Hamoadim: Parshat Moadei Yisrael*. Vol. II: *Shalosh Regalim, Pesaḥ*. Tel Aviv, n.d. [1966?].
Becker, Ph[ilipp] Aug[ust]. "Von den Erzählern neben und nach Chrestien de Troyes," *Zeitschrift für romanische Philologie*, LV (1935), 385-445.
Ben-Ezra, E. "*Minhagei Hasedarim*," *Hadoar* (Nisan 5711-April 1951), 471.
Ben-Yaakov, Avraham, ed. *Yalkut Minhagim*. Jerusalem, 1967.
———. "*Miminhagei Yahadut Bavel*," *Yalkut Minhagim*. Jerusalem, 1967, pp. 13-42.
Bezzola, Reto Roberto. *Les Origines et la formation de la littérature courtoise en occident (500-1200)*. 3 vols. Paris, 1944-63.
———. *Le Sens de l'aventure et de l'amour (Chrétien de Troyes)*. Paris, 1947.

Blau, Joshua. *The Emergence and Linguistic Background of Judaeo-Arabic.* Scripta Judaica, V. Oxford, 1965.

Blondheim, David Simon. *Contribution à la lexicographie française d'après des sources rabbiniques* (Doctoral Dissertation, The John Hopkins University, June, 1910), Paris, 1910. Extrait de la Romania XXXIX (1910), 129-183.

———. *Les Gloses françaises dans les commentaires talmudiques de Raschi. Tome Deux: Etudes lexicographiques,* The John Hopkins Studies in Romance Languages and Literatures, Extra Vol. II, Baltimore, 1937.

Blumenkranz, Bernhard. "France From the First Settlement until the Revolution." *Encyclopedia Judaica.* Jerusalem, 1972, VII, 7-22.

Boehmer, Eduard. "De Vocabulis Francogallicis Judice transcriptis," *Romanische Studien,* I (1871-75), 197-220.

Bormann, Ernst. *Die Jagd in den altenfranzösischen Artus-und-Abenteur-Romanen.* Ausgaben und Abhandlungen aus dem Gebiete der Romanischen Philologie, LXVIII. Marburg, 1887.

Brogyanyi, Gabriel John. "Will and Motivation in the Romances of Chrétien de Troyes." Thesis, Cornell University, 1969.

Brown, Arthur C. L. *The Origin of the Grail Legend.* Cambridge, Mass., 1943.

Bruce, James Douglas. *The Evolution of Arthurian Romance from the Beginnings Down to the Year 1300.* 2 vols. Göttingen, 1923.

Bultmann, Rudolf. "Prophesy and Fulfillment," *Essays in Old Testament Hermaneutics,* ed. Claus Westermann, tr. James Luther Mays. Richmond, Va., 1967.

Burdach, Konrard. *Der Gral: Forschungen über seinen Ursprung und seinen Zusammenhang mit der Longinuslegende,* Forschungen zur Kirchen-und Geistesgeschichte, XIV. Stuttgart, 1938.

———. "Theologie und Kirchenwesen," *Deutsche Literaturzeitung,* XXIV (1903), cols. 3050-3058.

———. "Zum Ursprung der Salomo-Sage," *Archiv für das Studium der neueren Spachen und Literaturen.* CVIII (1902), 121-132.

Cassel, Paulus. *Der Gral und sein Name,* 2nd ed. Berlin, 1878.

Castiglioni, Vittore. "Italy," *The Jewish Encyclopedia,* New York, 1910. VII, 1-11.

Chamberlin, E[ric] R[ussell]. *Life in Medieval France.* European Life Series, ed. Peter Quenell. London, 1967.

Charity, A. C. *Events and their Afterlife. The Dialectics of Christian Typology in the Bible and Dante.* Cambridge, England, 1966.

Chew, Samuel Claggett. *The Pilgrimage of Life. An Exploration into the Renaissance Mind.* New Haven, 1962.

Colby, Alice M. *The Portrait in Twelfth-Century French Literature: An Example of the Stylistic Originality of Chrétien de Troyes.* Geneva, 1965.

Coulet, Henri. *Histoire du roman en France.* Vol. I: *Le Roman jusqu'à la révolution.* Collection U, "Lettres françaises." Paris, 1967.

Daniélou, Jean, S. J. *From Shadows to Reality,* tr. Wulstan Hibberd. London, 1960.

Daniélou, Jean. *Sacramentum futuri: Etudes sur les origines de la typologie biblique.* Paris, 1950.

Danino, Shalom. "Miminhagei Yahadut Maroko," *Yalkut Minhagim,* ed. Avraham Ben Yaakov. Jerusalem, 1967, pp. 100-130.

Darmesteter, Arsène. "L'Autodafé de Troyes de 1288," *Revue des Etudes Juives*, II (1881), 199-246.
———. "L'Autodafé de Troyes (24 avril 1288)," *Arsène Darmesteter: Reliques scientifiques*, I, 217-264.
———. "Deux Elégies du Vatican," *Reliques scientifiques*, I, 265-307, and *Romania*, III (1874), 443-486.
———. "Gloses et glossaires hébreux-français du moyen âge," *Reliques scientifiques*, I, 165-195.
———. "Rapport sur une Mission en Italie," *Reliques scientifiques*, I, 119-164.
———. "Rapport sur une mission en Angletaire," *Reliques scientifiques*, I, 107-118.
———. *Reliques scientifiques recueillies par son frère*. 2 vols. Paris, 1890.
Darmesteter, Arsène and Blondheim, D[avid] S[imon]. *Les Gloses françaises dans les commentaires talmudiques de Raschi*. Tome Premier: *Texte des Gloses*, Bibliothèque de l'Ecole des Hautes Etudes, Fasc. 254, Paris, 1945.
Davies, W. D. *The Setting of the Sermon on the Mount*. Cambridge, 1964.
Dillon, Myles. *Early Irish Literature*. Chicago, 1948.
Du Sommerand, Alexandre. *Les Arts au Moyen Age*, Album of Plates, Vol. II, Series 4. Paris, 1838.
Eisenstein, J. D. *Otzar Peirushim Vetziyurim el Haggadah Shel Pesaḥ*. New York, 1920.
Faral, Edmond. *La Vie quotidienne au temps de Saint Louis*. Paris, 1938.
Federbursh, Simon, ed. *Rashi: His Teachings and Personality. Essays on the Occasion of the 850th Anniversary of his Death*. New York, 1958.
Fourrier, Anthime. "Encore la chronologie des œuvres de Chrétien de Troyes," *Bulletin bibliographique de la Société Internationale Arthurienne*, II (1950), 69-88.
Fowler, David C. *Prowess and Charity in the Perceval of Chrétien de Troyes*. Seattle, 1959.
Frappier, Jean. "Autres remarques sur le vers 3301 du Conte du Graal," *Bulletin bibliographique de la Société Internationale Arthurienne*, II (1950), 89-93.
———. *Chrétien de Troyes: l'homme et l'œuvre*, Connaissance des Lettres L. Paris, 1957.
———. "Du 'Graal trestot descovert' à la forme du Graal chez Chrétien de Troyes," *Romania*, LXXIII (1952), 82-92.
———. "Du 'Graal trestot descovert' à l'origine de la légende," *Romania*, LXXIV (1953), 358-375.
———. "Encore le 'Graal trestot descovert'," *Romania*, LXXII (1951), 236-238.
———. "Le 'Conte du Graal' est-il une allégorie judéo-chrétienne?," I, *Romance Philology*, XVI (1962), 179-213; II, *Romance Philology*, XX (1966), 1-31.
———. "Le Graal et l'Hostie [*Conte del Graal*, v. 6413-6431]," *Les Romans du Graal*, pp. 63-82.
———. *Le Roman breton: Perceval ou le Conte du Graal*, "Les Cours de Sorbonne." Paris, 1966.
———. "Note complémentaire sur la composition du 'Conte du Graal'," *Romania*, LXXXI (1960), 308-337.
———. "Sur l'interprétation du vers 3301 du *Conte du Graal*," *Romania*, LXXI (1950), 240-246.

Gaster, T. H. *Passover: Its History and Tradition*. New York, 1949.
Ginzberg, Louis. *The Legends of the Jews*. 7 vols. Philadelphia, 1909-1938.
Glenn, Menaḥem G. "On Rashi's Life and Teachings," *Rashi*, ed. S. Federbush, pp. 131-155.
Glorieux, P[almeon]. *Pour revaloriser Migne: Tables rectificatives*. Mélanges de Science Religieuse, IXe Année, Cahier Supplémentaire. Lille, 1952.
Goldin, Hyman E. *A Treasury Of Jewish Holidays*. New York, 1952.
Goodman, Philip, ed. *The Passover Anthology*. Philadelphia, 1961.
Grayzel, Solomon. *A History of the Jews from the Babylonian Exile to the Present*. Philadelphia, 1968.
Gutmann, Joseph. *Jewish Ceremonial Art*. New York, 1964.
Haidu, Peter. *Aesthetic Distance in Chrétien de Troyes: Irony and Comedy in Cligès and Perceval*. Geneva, 1968.
Hatzfeld, Helmut A. "Esthetic Criticism Applied to Medieval Romance Literature," *Romance Philology*, I (1947-48), 305-327.
Hebert, Gabriel. *When Israel came out of Egypt*. Richmond, Va., 1961.
Heinzel, Richard. *Ueber die französichen Gralromane*, Denkschriften der Kaiserlichen Akademie der Wissenschaften, Philosophisch-historische Classe, XI, pt. 3. Vienna, 1892.
Hofer, Stefan. *Chrétien de Troyes: Leben und Werke des altfranzösischen Epikers*. Graz-Köln, 1954.
Holmes, Urban T[igner], Jr. *Chrétien de Troyes*. New York, 1970.
———. *A New Interpretation of Chrétien's Conte del Graal*. University of North Carolina Studies in the Romance Languages and Literatures, VIII. Chapel Hill, 1948.
Holmes, Urban T[igner], Jr. and Sister M. Amelia Klenke, O.P. *Chrétien, Troyes and the Grail*. Chapel Hill, 1959.
"The Holy Grail," *Encyclopedia Britannica*, Chicago, 1968, X, 659.
Huizinga, J[ohan]. *The Waning of the Middle Ages*. Garden City, New York, 1949.
Imbs, Paul. "L'Elément religieux dans le Conte del Graal de Chrétien de Troyes," *Les Romans du Graal*, Paris, 1956, pp. 31-62.
Jackson, Kenneth. "Les sources celtiques du Roman du Graal," *Les Romans du Graal*, Paris, 1956, pp. 213-232.
Jodogne, Omer. "L'Autre Monde celtique dans la littérature française du XIIe siècle," *Bulletin de la Classe des Lettres et des Sciences morales et politiques de l'Académie royale de Belgique*, 5th series, XLVI (1960), 584-597.
Johnson, E. "Easter and its Cycle," *New Catholic Encyclopedia*, ed. Catholic University of America. New York, 1967, V, 6-9.
Kahane, Henry and Renée. "Proto-Perceval and Proto-Parzival," *Zeitschrift für Romanische Philologie*, LXXIX (1963), 335-342.
———. "On the Sources of Chrétien's *Grail Story*," *Festschrift Walther von Wartburg zum 80. Geburtstage* (v. no. 18), I, 191-233.
Kahane, Henry and Renée and Pietrangeli, Angelina. *The Krater and the Grail: Hermetic Sources of the Parzival*. Urbana, 1965.
Kaminka, Armand. "Benjamin of Tudela," *The Universal Jewish Encyclopedia*, New York, 1940. II, 180.
Kayserling, Meyer. "Sephardim," *The Jewish Encyclopedia*. New York, 1901. XI, 197-198.

Kellermann, Wilhelm. *Aufbaustil und Weltbild Chrestien von Troyes im Percevalroman.* Beihefte zur Zeitschrift für romanische Philologie, LXXXVIII. Halle, 1936.
Kittredge, George Lyman. "To take Time by the Forelook," *Modern Language Notes,* VIII (1893), 230-235.
Klenke, Sister M. Amelia, O. P. *Liturgy and Allegory in Chrétien's "Perceval."* University of North Carolina Studies in the Romance Languages and Literatures, XIV. Chapel Hill, 1951.
Knott, Eleanor and Murphy, Gerard. *Early Irish Literature.* New York, 1966.
Köhler, E[rich]. "Diskussion uber die Einheit von Chrestiens 'Li Conte del Graal'," *Zeitschrift für romanische Philologie,* LXXXIX (1959), 523-529.
———. "Les Romans de Chrétien de Troyes," *Revue de l'Institut de Sociologie,* XXXVI (1963), 271-284.
Landsberger, Frantz. "The Cincinnati Haggadah and its Decorator," *Hebrew Union College Annual,* XV (1940), 529-558.
Lanson, G[ustave] and Truffau, Paul. *Histoire de la littérature française, remaniée et complétée pour la période 1850-1950 par Paul Truffau.* Paris, 1955.
Learsi, Rufus (Israel Goldberg). *Israel: A History of the Jewish People.* Cleveland, 1949.
Leclerq, H. "Calice," *Dictionnaire d'archéologie chrétienne et de la liturgie.* Paris, 1910. II, col. 608.
. Lehrmann, C. *L'Elément juif dans la littérature française.* 2 vols. Présences du judaisme. Paris, 1960.
Lévi, Israel. "France," *The Jewish Encyclopedia,* New York, 1964, V, 442-463.
Liber, Maurice. *Rashi,* tr. Adele Szold. Philadelphia, 1906.
Lipschuetz, Eliezer Meir. *Rashi, Rabbi Shelomoh Yitzḥaki* (in Hebrew). Jerusalem, 1966.
Loomis, Laura Hibbard. "The Passion Lance Relic and the War Cry Monjoie in the Chanson de Roland and Related Texts," *Romanic Review,* XLI (1950), 241-260.
Loomis, Roger Sherman. *Arthurian Tradition and Chrétien de Troyes.* New York, 1949.
———. "By What Route did the Romantic Tradition of Arthur Reach the French?," *Modern Philology,* XXXIII (1936), 225-238.
———. "Les Légendes hagiographes et la légende du Graal," *Les Romans du Graal.* Paris, 1956.
———. *The Grail: From Celtic Myth to Christian Symbol.* Cardiff and New York, 1963.
———. "The Irish Origin of the Grail Legend," *Speculum,* VIII (1933), 415-430.
Lot-Borodine, Myrrha. "Autour du saint Graal: A propos de travaux récents," *Romania,* LVII (1931), 147-205.
Lubelsky, Mordecai. "At a Seder in Casablanca," *The Sunday Review, The Day Jewish Journal* (April 20, 1958), III, 4.
Mangenot, E. "Exode," *Dictionnaire de Théologie catholique contenant l'exposé des doctrines de la théologie catholique, leurs prières et leur histoire.* Eds. A. Vacant and E. Mangenot. Paris, 1913, V.
Mâle, Emile. *L'Art religieux du XIIe au XVIIIe siècle. Extraits choisis par l'auteur.* 2nd ed. Paris, 1946.

Margoliouth, G[eorge]. *Catalogue of the Hebrew and Samaritan Manuscripts in the British Museum.* Vol. II. London, 1965.
Marx, Jean. *La Légende arthurienne et le Graal.* Paris, 1952.
———. *Nouvelles Recherches sur la littérature arthurienne,* Bibliothèque française et romane, Series C, Etudes Littéraires, IX. Paris, 1965.
Matzke, J. E. "On the Source of the Italian and English Idioms Meaning 'To take Time by the Forelock'," *PMLA,* VIII (1893), 303-334.
Metzger, Mendel. "La Haggada enluminée." 4 vols. Thesis, University of Poitiers, 1961. Bibliothèque Universitaire de Poitiers 350-728 5-1961. Bibliothèque du Centre d'Etudes Supérieures de Civilisation Médiévale, Université de Poitiers: I. 1961. I (vols. 1 and 2 only).
———. *La Haggada enluminée.* Vol. I: *Etude iconographique et stylistique des manuscrits enluminés et décorés de la Haggada du XIIIe au XVIe siècle.* Etudes sur le judaïsme médiéval, II. Leiden, 1973.
Micha, A. "Deux études sur le graal, I: Le Graal et la Lance," *Romania,* LXXIII (1952), 462-479.
Mikliszanski, I. K. "Ḥayyei Hamoreh," *Rashi,* ed. S. Federbush, pp. 13-30.
Misrahi, Jean. "New Light on the Chronology of Chrétien de Troyes?," *Bulletin bibliographique de la Société Internationale Arthurienne,* XI (1959), 89-120.
Neale, J[ohn] M[ason]. *History of the Eastern Church.* London, 1850.
Neuman, Abraham A. "Sephardim," *The Universal Jewish Encyclopedia.* New York, 1943. IX, 477-478.
Neubauer, Adolphe. "Un Vocabulaire hébraïco-français," *Romanische Studien,* I (1871-75), 163-196.
Newstead, Helaine. *Bran the Blessed in Arthurian Romance.* New York, 1939.
Nichols, Stephen G., Jr. "The Interaction of Life and Literature in the *Peregrinationes ad Loca Sancta* and the *Chansons de Geste,*" *Speculum,* XLIV (169), 51-72.
Nitze, William A. "Le Bruiden, Le château du Graal, et la lance-qui-saigne," *Les Romans du Graal.* Paris, 1956, pp. 279-296.
Nutt, Alfred. *The Legend of the Holy Grail with Especial Reference to the Hypothesis of Its Celtic Origin.* London, 1888.
Olschki, Leonardo. *The Grail Castle and its Mysteries,* tr. J. A. Scott, ed. Eugène Vinaver. Manchester, 1966.
Owen, D. D. R. *The Evolution of the Grail Legend,* St. Andrews Univ. Publications, LVIII. Edinburgh and London, 1968.
Parfaict, E. and C. *Histoire du théâtre français depuis son origine jusqu'à présent.* Vol. II. Paris, 1745.
Parry, Thomas. *A History of Welsh Literature,* tr. H. Idris Bell. Oxford, 1955.
Patch, Howard R. *The Goddess Fortuna in Mediaeval Literature.* Cambridge, Mass., 1927.
Pauphilet, Albert. "Au sujet du Graal," *Romania,* LXVI (1940-41), 289-321; 481-504.
———. *Le Legs du Moyen Age.* Melun, 1950.
Peebles, Rose J. *The Legend of Longinus and its Connection with the Grail.* Baltimore, 1911.
Pietsch, Karl, "On the Source of 'To take Time by the Forelock'," *Modern Language Notes,* VIII (1893), 235-338.

Pollmann, Leo. *Chrétien de Troyes und der 'Conte del Graal.'* Beihefte zur Zeitschrift für romanische Philologie, c. Tübingen, 1965.

Riquer, M[artín] de. "La composición de 'Li contes del Graal'," *Boletín de la Real Academia de Buenas Letras de Barcelona,* XXVII (157-58), 279-320.

———. "Perceval y Gauvin en 'Li contes del Graal'," *Filologica Romanza,* IV (1957), 119-147.

Roach, William. "Eucharistic Tradition in the Perlesvaus," *Zeitschrift für romanische Philologie,* LIX (1939), 10-56.

Roques, Mario. *Le Graal de Chrétien et la Demoiselle au Graal.* Publications Romanes et Françaises, L. Geneva, 1955.

Les Romans du Graal dans la littérature des XIIe et XIIIe siècles. Colloques Internationaux du Centre National de la Recherche Scientifique, III, Strasbourg, 29 mars-3 avril 1954. Paris, 1956.

Satbon, Mordekhai and Tal, Avraham. "*Miminhagei Yahadut Tunisia,*" *Yalkut Minhagim,* ed. Avraham Ben-Yaakov. Jerusalem, 1967, pp. 131-151.

Saulnier, V. L. *La Littérature française du moyen âge.* 7th ed. "Que Sais-je?" CXLV. Paris, 1967.

Schauss, Ḥayyim. *Guide to Jewish Holy Days: History and Observances,* tr. Samuel Jaffe. New York, 1961.

Segal, J. B. *The Hebrew Passover from the Earliest Times to A.D. 70.* London, 1963.

Siffrin, Pietro. "Patena," *Enciclopedia Cattolica.* Vatican, 1948-54, IX, 939.

Singleton, Charles S. "In Exitu Israel de Aegypto," *Dante: A Collection of Critical Essays,* ed. John Freccero. Englewood Cliffs, N.J., 1965, pp. 102-121.

Slouschz, Nahum. *Travels in North Africa.* Philadelphia, 1927.

Smalley, Beryl. *The Study of the Bible in the Middle Ages.* 2nd ed. New York, 1952.

Southern, Richard William. *The Making of the Middle Ages.* New Haven, 1953.

Stowell, William Averill. *Old-French Titles of Respect in Direct Address.* Baltimore, 1908.

Swainson, C. A. *The Greek Liturgies.* Cambridge, England, 1884.

Synan, Edward A. *The Popes and the Jews in the Middle Ages.* New York, 1967.

Tabak, Israel. "Rashi and the Non-Jewish World," *Rashi,* ed. S. Federbush, pp. 107-111.

Trens, M. *La Eucaristia en el arte español.* Barcelona, 1952.

Tucker, Dunston J. "In Exitu Israel de Aegypto: The *Divine Comedy* in Light of the Easter Liturgy," *The American Benedictine Review.* IX (1960), 43-61.

Vendryès, J. "Les Eléments celtiques de la légende du Graal," *Etudes Celtiques,* V (1949), 1-50.

———. "Remarques sur la communication de M. Jackson," *Les Romans du Graal,* pp. 227-228.

Weinberger, R. M. "Pesaḥ im Yehudei Paras," *Hadoar* (Nisan, 5707, April, 1947), p. 554.

Werblowsky, R. J. Zwi, and Wigoder, Geoffrey, eds. *The Encyclopedia of Jewish Religion.* Jerusalem and Tel Aviv, 1966.

Weston, Jessie. *From Ritual to Romance.* Cambridge, England, 1920.

———. *The Legend of Sir Perceval: Studies upon its Origin, Development and Position in the Arthurian Cycle.* 2 vols. London, 1906-09.

Weinraub, Eugene J. "Chrétien's Grail: A Jewish Rite? A New Investigation based upon Medieval Hebraic Sources." Thesis, Cornell University, 1970. University Microfilms; Ann Arbor, Michigan, Reorder No. 71-1081.

———. "Chrétien's Grail: A Jewish Rite? A New Investigation Based Upon Medieval Hebraic Sources" *Dissertation Abstracts International* XXXI (1971), 4738A.

———. "Chrétien's Grail: A Jewish Rite? A New Investigation Based Upon Medieval Hebraic Sources (Daniel Potier)," *Cahiers de Civilisation Médiévale,* XIV (1971), 399-401.

Wischnitzer, Rachel. "Passover In Art," *The Passover Anthology,* ed. Philip Goodman. Philadelphia, 1961, pp. 295-324.

Yaari, Abraham. *Bibliography of the Passover Haggadah from the Earliest Printed Edition to 1960.* Jerusalem, 1960.

Zenner, Walter P. "Syrian Jews in Three Social Settings," *The Jewish Journal of Sociology,* X (1968), 101-120.

Zimmerls, H. J. *Ashkenazim and Sephardim: Their Relations, Differences and Problems as Reflected in the Rabbinical Responsa.* London, 1958.

Zuartz, Frija. "*Miminhagei Yahadut Luv,*" *Yalkut Mihagim,* ed. Avraham Ben-Yaakov. Jerusalem, 1967, pp. 74-99.

Zumthor, Paul. "Toujours à propos de la date du Conte del Graal," *Le Moyen Age,* LXV, 4th Series, XIV (1959), 579-586.

Modern Dictionaries

Ben-Yehudah, Eliezer, ed. *A Complete Dictionary of Ancient and Modern Hebrew by Eliezer Ben Yehuda of Jerusalem.* 16 vols. Jerusalem and New York, 1940-1959.

Douglas, J. D. *The New Bible Dictionary.* Grand Rapids, 1962.

Dozy, Reinhart Pieter Anne. *Supplément aux Dictionnaires Arabes.* 2 vols. Leiden, Paris, 1877.

Foerster, Wendelin. *Kristian von Troyes: Wörterbuch zu seinen sämtlichen Werken.* Halle, 1914.

Foerster, Wendelin and Breuer, Hermann. *Wörterbuch zu Kristian von Troyes sämtlichen Werken.* 3rd ed. Tübingen, 1964.

Foulet, Lucien. *Glossary of the First Continuation,* Vol. III, pt. 2. *The Continuation of the Old French Perceval of Chrétien de Troyes,* ed. William Roach. Philadelphia, 1955.

Gaskell, G[eorge] A[rthur]. *Dictionary of all Scriptures and Myths.* New York, 1960.

Godefroy, Frédéric. *Dictionnaire de l'ancienne langue française du XIe au XVe siècle.* 10 vols. Paris, 1880-1902.

Grandsaignes d'Hauterive, R. *Dictionnaire d'ancien français: Moyen Age et Renaissance.* Paris, 1947.

Gross, Henri. *Gallia Judaica: Dictionnaire géographique de la France d'après les sources rabbiniques,* tr. Moïse Bloch. Paris, 1897.

Jastrow, Marcus. *A Dictionary of the Targumim, the Talmud Babli and Yerushalmi, and the Midrashic Literature.* 2 vols. New York, 1950.

Kazimirski, Albin. *Dictionnaire arabe-français.* 2 vols. Paris, 1860.
Lane, Edward William. *An Arabic-English Lexicon.* Book I. 6 vols. London, 1863-1893.
Levy, Jacob. *Neuhebräisches und chaldäisches Wörterbuch über die Talmudim und Midraschim.* 4 vols. Leipzig, 1876-1889.
Levy, Raphael. *Trésor de la langue des Juifs français au moyen âge.* Austin, 1964.
Tobler, Adolf, and Lommatzsch, Erhard. *Altfranzösisches Wörterbuch.* 7 vols. and facs. A-raier. Berlin, Wiesbaden, 1925-1969.
Vacant, A., Mangenot, E. and Amann, E., eds. *Dictionnaire de théologie catholique contenant l'exposé des doctrines de la théologie catholique, leurs prières et leur histoire.* 15 vols. Paris, 1903-1946.
Wartburg, Walther von. *Französisches etymologisches Wörterbuch.* 17 vols. Bonn, Basel, 1928-1966.
Wehr, Hans. *A Dictionary of Modern Written Arabic,* ed. J. Milton Cowan. Second Printing. Ithaca, New York, 1966.
Wilson, Walter Lewis. *Wilson's Dictionary of Bible Types.* Grand Rapids, 1957.

Personal Interviews

Conducted with Messrs. Franklin Beda, Saul Tawil, and Samuel Sutton of the Syrian Jewish Community of Brooklyn, New York (Congregation Shaare Zion).

TABLE OF PLATES

Plate   *Page*

1. The Simple Son and the Son Who Knows Not How to Ask. From a fourteenth-century *Haggadah* of Provençal or Spanish provenance. Private collection (Ernst Daniel Goldschmidt, *The Passover Haggadah: Its Sources and History* [Jerusalem, 1961], VII) ... ...   facing page   5

2. Family *Seder* scene. From the fourteenth-century *Sarajevo Haggadah* (Cecil Roth. *The Sarajevo Haggadah* [New York, n.d.]) ... ...   facing page   15

3. Ha Laḥma Anya, "This is the bread of affliction". From the *Sarajevo Haggadah* (Y.L. Barukh and Yom-Tov Levinsky, *Sepher Hamoadim*, Vol. II: *Shalosh Regalim, Pesaḥ* [Tel Aviv, 1963], xxiii) Samaritan Paschal sacrifice (Barukh and Levinsky, *Sepher Hamoadim* II, xxiii)
The Passover sacrifice depicted on a *Seder* plate (Barukh and Levinsky, *Sepher Hamoadim*, II, xxiii) ... ...   following page   20

4. Perforating *matzot*. From a fifteenth-century *Haggadah* MS in the Münich Museum (Barukh and Levinsky, *Sepher Hamoadim* II, xx)
Haggadah fragments and *Seder* illustrations on a *Seder* plate (Barukh and Levinsky, *Sepher Hamoadim* II, xx) ... ...   following page   20

5. *Seder* plate. Faience. Pesaro, Italy. Dated 1614 (Philip Goodman, *The Passover Anthology* [Philadelphia, 1961], plate 24) ... ...   following page   32

6. *Seder* plate. Majolica. Ancona, Italy. 1673 (Goodman, *The Passover Anthology*, plate 25) ... ...   following page   32

7. Passover plate. Pewter. Master G. R. van Go. Dated 1718. Engraved decoration dated 1808 (Goodman, *The Passover Anthology*, plate 26) ...   following page   50

8. Passover plate. Pewter. Alsace-Lorraine. Eighteenth-century (Goodman, *The Passover Anthology*, plate 29) ... ...   following page   50

Plate		Page
9.	Passover plate. Pewter. 1773. Made by Baruch Schechter of Fuerth for Jacob Cohen (Goodman, *The Passover Anthology*, plate 28)	following page 88
10.	*Seder* plate. Silver repoussé work. Hanau, Germany. Nineteenth century (Goodman, *The Passover Anthology*, plate 30)	following page 88
11.	*Seder* Night. A painting by Moritz Oppenheim (1799-1822) illustrating an Ashkenazic. Seder (Barukh and Levinsky *Sepher Hamoadim*, II, xvii).	following page 102
12.	A Marrano *Seder* (Barukh and Levinsky, *Sepher Hamoadim*, II, xix) A Model *Seder* in the Israel Defense Forces	following page 102
13.	Procession with Symbolic Passover Foods. (*Haggadah, British Museum Add. 14761*. 14th century, Spanish)	following page 116

NORTH CAROLINA STUDIES IN THE ROMANCE LANGUAGES AND LITERATURES

I.S.B.N. Prefix 0-88438

Recent Titles

CHARLES NODIER: HIS LIFE AND WORKS, by Sarah Fore Bell. 1971. (No. 95). -895-6.
RACINE AND SENECA, by Ronald W. Tobin. 1971. (No. 96). -896-4.
LOPE DE VEGA. "EL PEREGRINO EN SU PATRIA," edición de Myron A. Peyton. 1971. (No. 97), -897-2.
CRITICAL REACTIONS AND THE CHRISTIAN ELEMENT IN THE POETRY OF PIERRE DE RONSARD, by Mark S. Whitney. 1971. (No. 98). -898-0.
THE REV. JOHN BOWLE. THE GENESIS OF CERVANTEAN CRITICISM, by Ralph Merritt Cox. 1971. (No. 99). -899-9.
THE FOUR INTERPOLATED STORIES IN THE "ROMAN COMIQUE": THEIR SOURCES AND UNIFYING FUNCTION, by Frederick Alfed De Armas. 1971. (No. 100). -900-6.
LE CHASTOIEMENT D'UN PERE A SON FILS, A CRITICAL EDITION, edited by Edward D. Montgomery, Jr. 1971. (No. 101). -901-4.
LE ROMMANT DE "GUY DE WARWIK" ET DE "HEROLT D'ARDENNE," edited by D. J. Conlon. 1971. (No. 102). -902-2.
THE OLD PORTUGUESE "VIDA DE SAM BERNARDO," EDITED FROM ALCOBAÇA MANUSCRIPT ccxci/200, WITH INTRODUCTION, LINGUISTIC STUDY, NOTES, TABLE OF PROPER NAMES, AND GLOSSARY, by Lawrence A. Sharpe. 1971. (No. 103). -903-0.
A CRITICAL AND ANNOTATED EDITION OF LOPE DE VEGA'S "LAS ALMENAS DE TORO," by Thomas E. Case. 1971. (No. 104). -904-9.
LOPE DE VEGA'S "LO QUE PASA EN UNA TARDE," A CRITICAL, ANNOTATED EDITION OF THE AUTOGRAPH MANUSCRIPT, by Richard Angelo Picerno. 1971. (No. 105). -905-7.
OBJECTIVE METHODS FOR TESTING AUTHENTICITY AND THE STUDY OF TEN DOUBTFUL "COMEDIAS" ATTRIBUTED TO LOPE DE VEGA, by Fred M. Clark. 1971. (No. 106). -906-5.
THE ITALIAN VERB. A MORPHOLOGICAL STUDY, by Frede Jensen. 1971. (No. 107). -907-3.
A CRITICAL EDITION OF THE OLD PROVENÇAL EPIC "DAUREL ET BETON," WITH NOTES AND PROLEGOMENA, by Arthur S. Kimmel. 1971. (No. 108). -908-1.
FRANCISCO RODRIGUES LOBO: DIALOGUE AND COURTLY LORE IN RENAISSANCE PORTUGAL, by Richard A. Preto-Rodas. 1971. (No. 109). 909-X.
RAIMOND VIDAL: POETRY AND PROSE, edited by W. H. W. Field. 1971. (No. 110). -910-3.
RELIGIOUS ELEMENTS IN THE SECULAR LYRICS OF THE TROUBADOURS, by Raymond Gay-Crosier. 1971. (No. 111). -911-1.
THE SIGNIFICANCE OF DIDEROT'S "ESSAI SUR LE MERITE ET LA VERTU," by Gordon B. Walters. 1971. (No. 112). -912-X.
PROPER NAMES IN THE LYRICS OF THE TROUBADOURS, by Frank M. Chambers. 1971. (No. 113). -913-8.
STUDIES IN HONOR OF MARIO A. PEI, edited by John Fisher and Paul A. Gaeng. 1971. (No. 114). -914-6.
DON MANUEL CAÑETE, CRONISTA LITERARIO DEL ROMANTICISMO Y DEL POSROMANTICISMO EN ESPAÑA, por Donald Allen Randolph. 1972. (No. 115). -915-4.
THE TEACHINGS OF SAINT LOUIS. A CRITICAL TEXT, by David O'Connell. 1972. (No. 116). -916-2.
HIGHER, HIDDEN ORDER: DESIGN AND MEANING IN THE ODES OF MALHERBE, by David Lee Rubin. 1972. (No. 117). -917-0.
JEAN DE LE MOTE "LE PARFAIT DU PAON," édition critique par Richard J. Carey. 1972. (No. 118). -918-9.
CAMUS' HELLENIC SOURCES, by Paul Archambault. 1972. (No. 119). -919-7.

Recent Titles

FROM VULGAR LATIN TO OLD PROVENÇAL, by Frede Jensen. 1972. (No. 120). *-920-0*.

GOLDEN AGE DRAMA IN SPAIN: GENERAL CONSIDERATION AND UNUSUAL FEATURES, by Sturgis E. Leavitt. 1972. (No. 121). *-921-9*.

THE LEGEND OF THE "SIETE INFANTES DE LARA" (*Refundición toledana de la crónica de 1344* versión), study and edition by Thomas A. Lathrop. 1972. (No. 122). *-922-7*.

STRUCTURE AND IDEOLOGY IN BOIARDO'S "ORLANDO INNAMORATO," by Andrea di Tommaso. 1972. (No. 123). *-923-5*.

STUDIES IN HONOR OF ALFRED G. ENGSTROM, edited by Robert T. Cargo and Emmanuel J. Mickel, Jr. 1972. (No. 124). *-924-3*.

A CRITICAL EDITION WITH INTRODUCTION AND NOTES OF GIL VICENTE'S "FLORESTA DE ENGANOS," by Constantine Christopher Stathatos. 1972. (No. 125). *-925-1*.

LI ROMANS DE WITASSE LE MOINE. *Roman du treizième siècle*. Édité d'après le manuscrit, fonds français 1553, de la Bibliothèque Nationale, Paris, par Denis Joseph Conlon. 1972. (No. 126). *-926-X*.

EL CRONISTA PEDRO DE ESCAVIAS. *Una vida del Siglo XV*, por Juan Bautista Avalle-Arce. 1972. (No. 127). *-927-8*.

AN EDITION OF THE FIRST ITALIAN TRANSLATION OF THE "CELESTINA," by Kathleen V. Kish. 1973. (No. 128). *-928-6*.

MOLIÈRE MOCKED. THREE CONTEMPORARY HOSTILE COMEDIES: *Zélinde, Le portrait du peintre, Élomire Hypocondre*, by Frederick Wright Vogler. 1973. (No. 129). *-929-4*.

C.-A. SAINTE-BEUVE. *Chateaubriand et son groupe littéraire sous l'empire*. Index alphabétique et analytique établi par Lorin A. Uffenbeck. 1973. (No. 130). *-930-8*.

THE ORIGINS OF THE BAROQUE CONCEPT OF "PEREGRINATIO," by Juergen Hahn. 1973. (No. 131). *-931-6*.

THE "AUTO SACRAMENTAL" AND THE PARABLE IN SPANISH GOLDEN AGE LITERATURE, by Donald Thaddeus Dietz. 1973. (No. 132). *-932-4*.

FRANCISCO DE OSUNA AND THE SPIRIT OF THE LETTER, by Laura Calvert. 1973. (No. 133). *-933-2*.

ITINERARIO DI AMORE: DIALETTICA DI AMORE E MORTE NELLA VITA NUOVA, by Margherita de Bonfils Templer. 1973. (No. 134). *-934-0*.

L'IMAGINATION POETIQUE CHEZ DU BARTAS: ELEMENTS DE SENSIBILITE BAROQUE DANS LA "CREATION DU MONDE," by Bruno Braunrot. 1973. (No. 135). *-934-0*.

ARTUS DESIRE: PRIEST AND PAMPHLETEER OF THE SIXTEENTH CENTURY, by Frank S. Giese. 1973. (No. 136). *-936-7*.

JARDIN DE NOBLES DONZELLAS, FRAY MARTIN DE CORDOBA, by Harriet Goldberg. 1974. (No. 137). *-937-5*.

Symposia

LOS NARRADORES HISPANOAMERICANOS DE HOY, edited by Juan Bautista Avalle-Arce. 1973. (No. 1). *-951-0*.

When ordering please cite the *ISBN Prefix* plus the last four digits for each title.

Send orders to:
    University of North Carolina Press
    Chapel Hill
    North Carolina 27514
    U. S. A.

The Department of Romance Studies Digital Arts and Collaboration Lab at the University of North Carolina at Chapel Hill is proud to support the digitization of the North Carolina Studies in the Romance Languages and Literatures series.

www.ingramcontent.com/pod-product-compliance
Ingram Content Group UK Ltd.
Pitfield, Milton Keynes, MK11 3LW, UK
UKHW041111021225
465592UK00002B/143